CARI

Shakespeare's Lost Play Re-imagined

NICK HERN BOOKS
London
www.nickhernbooks.co.uk

GREGORY DORAN

Gregory Doran is Chief Associate Director for the Royal Shakespeare Company. His work as a director for the company includes *Cardenio*, *Morte D'Arthur, Twelfth Night, Love's Labour's Lost, Hamlet, A Midsummer Night's Dream, Antony and Cleopatra, The Rape of Lucrece, Venus and Adonis, Merry Wives the Musical, Coriolanus, A Midsummer Night's Dream, The Gunpowder Season* in 2005, *Sejanus: His Fall, The Canterbury Tales, Othello, All's Well That Ends Well, The Taming of the Shrew, The Tamer Tamed, The Winter's Tale, The Island Princess, Much Ado About Nothing, Timon of Athens, King John, All is True (Henry VIII), As You Like It, The Merchant of Venice, Oroonoko, The Odyssey, The Jacobeans Season* in 2002 (Olivier Award for Outstanding Achievement of the Year, 2003).

Other theatre includes *The Giant* (Hampstead Theatre, London); *The Merchant of Venice, Anjin: The English Samurai* (for Horipro in Tokyo); *The Real Inspector Hound* and *Black Comedy* (Donmar Warehouse/West End); *Mahler's Conversion* (Aldwych); *Titus Andronicus* (Market Theatre, Johannesburg/National Theatre Studio); *The Joker of Seville* (Boston/Trinidad); *Someone to Watch Over Me* (Theatr Clwyd); *The Importance of Being Earnest, Bedroom Farce, An Inspector Calls, Private Lives* (Century Theatre); *Long Day's Journey into Night, Waiting for Godot, The Norman Conquests* (Nottingham Playhouse).

Television includes Michael Wood's *In Search of Shakespeare, Midsummer Night's Dreaming*.

Film includes *Hamlet, Macbeth*.

His work as a writer includes *Shakespeare's Lost Play: Re-imagining* Cardenio *for the Royal Shakespeare Company, The Shakespeare Almanac, Woza Shakespeare!* (with Antony Sher).

ANTONIO ÁLAMO

Antonio Álamo is an award-winning playwright and novelist whose work is regularly performed internationally. He has been the Artistic Director of the Teatro Lope de Vega in Sevilla since 2004. Theatre includes *Los borrachos/'The Drunkards'* (Teatro Central) for which he won the Tirso de Molina Prize; *Los enfermos/'The Patients'* (La Abadia Theatre); *Yo, Satán/'I, Satan'* (Bellas Artes Theatre); *Caos/'Chaos'* (Alcázar Theatre); *En un lugar de la niebla/'Somewhere in the Mist'*, a contemporary view of *Don Quixote* (Festival de Almagro). Novels include *Breve historia de la inmortalidad/'A Brief History of Immortality'*; *Una buena idea/'A Good Idea'*.

ABOUT THE ROYAL SHAKESPEARE COMPANY

The Royal Shakespeare Company at Stratford-upon-Avon was formed in 1960 and gained its Royal Charter in 1961. This year we celebrate 50 years as a home for Shakespeare's work, the wider classical repertoire and new plays.

The founding Artistic Director Peter Hall created an ensemble theatre company of young actors and writers. The Company was led by Hall, Peter Brook and Michel Saint-Denis. The founding principles were threefold: the Company would embrace the freedom and power of Shakespeare's work, train and develop young actors and directors, and crucially, experiment in new ways of making theatre. There was a new spirit amongst this post-war generation and they intended to open up Shakespeare's plays as never before.

The Company has had a distinct personality from the beginning. The search for new forms of writing and directing was led by Peter Brook. He pushed writers to experiment. "Just as Picasso set out to capture a larger slice of the truth by painting a face with several eyes and noses, Shakespeare, knowing that man is living his everyday life and at the same time is living intensely in the invisible world of his thoughts and feelings, developed a method through which we can see at one and the same time the look on a man's face and the vibrations of his brain."

The breadth of Peter Hall's vision cannot be underplayed. In 1955 he had premiered Samuel Beckett's *Waiting for Godot* in a small theatre in London and it was like opening a window during a storm, the tumult of new ideas happening across Europe in art, theatre and literature came flooding into British theatre. But this new thinking needed nurturing, and in the quietude of this small market town, it became possible to make exciting breakthroughs in the work.

The inspiring team at the heart of the Company gave this work direction and momentum and the RSC became known for exhilarating performances of Shakespeare alongside new masterpiece plays such as *The Homecoming* and *Old Times* by Harold Pinter. This combination thrilled modern audiences.

Peter Hall's rigour on classical text is legendary, but he applied everything he learnt working on Beckett, and later on Harold Pinter, to his work on Shakespeare, and vice versa. This close and demanding relationship between writers from different eras became the fuel which powered the creativity of the RSC.

A rich and varied range of writers flowed into the company and continue to do so. These include: Edward Albee, Howard Barker, Edward Bond, Howard Brenton, Marina Carr, Caryl Churchill, Martin Crimp, David Edgar, Peter Flannery, David Greig, Tony Harrison, Dennis Kelly, Martin McDonagh, Rona Munro, Anthony Neilson, Harold Pinter, Stephen Poliakoff, Adriano Shaplin, Wole Soyinka, Tom Stoppard, debbie tucker green, Timberlake Wertenbaker and Roy Williams.

The history of the Royal Shakespeare Company has also been a history of theatre spaces and the impact they have on the theatre which can be made within them. The Other Place was established in 1975. The 400-seat Swan Theatre was added in 1986. The RSC's spaces have seen some of the most epic, challenging and era-defining theatre – Peter Brook's Beckettian *King Lear* with Paul Scofield in the title role, the *Theatre of Cruelty* season which premiered Peter Weiss' *Marat/Sade*, Trevor Nunn's studio *Macbeth* in The Other Place, Michael Boyd's restoration of ensemble with *The Histories Cycle* in The Courtyard Theatre, David Greig's and Roy Williams' searing war plays *The American Pilot* and *Days of Significance*, and most recently Dennis Kelly and Tim Minchin's game-changing musical adaptation of Roald Dahl's *Matilda*.

The Company today is led by Michael Boyd, who is taking its founding ideals forward. His belief in ensemble theatre-making, internationalism, new work and active approaches to Shakespeare in the classroom has inspired the Company to landmark projects such as *The Complete Works Festival*, *Stand up for Shakespeare* and *The Histories Cycle*. He has overseen the four year transformation of our theatres, he has restored the full range of repertoire and in this birthday year we are proud to invite the world's theatre artists onto our brand new stages.

NEW WORK AT THE RSC

The potential for new work at the RSC is something which we take very seriously. We have between thirty and forty writers working on new plays for us at any one time and have recently re-launched the RSC Studio to provide the resources for writers, directors and actors to explore and develop new ideas for our stages.

We believe that our writers help to establish a creative culture within the Company which both inspires new work and creates an ever more urgent sense of enquiry into the classics. The benefits work both ways. With our writers, our actors naturally learn the language of dramaturgical intervention and sharpen their interpretation of roles. Our writers benefit from re-discovering the stagecraft and theatre skills. They regain the knack of writing roles for leading actors. They become hungry to use classical structures to power up their plays.

Our current International Writer-in-Residence, Tarell Alvin McCraney has been embedded with the Company for two years. Whilst contributing creatively to the work of the Company's directors and actors he has also developed his own writing and theatre practice. His new play for the RSC, *American Trade*, will be performed by the Ensemble at Hampstead Theatre later this year. His post was funded by the CAPITAL Centre at the University of Warwick where he taught as part of his residency.

We invite writers to spend time with us in our rehearsal rooms, with our actors and practitioners. Alongside developing their own plays, we invite them to contribute dramaturgically to both our main stage Shakespeares and our Young People's Shakespeare.

The RSC Literary Department is generously supported by THE DRUE HEINZ TRUST

The RSC Ensemble is generously supported by THE GATSBY CHARITABLE FOUNDATION and THE KOVNER FOUNDATION.

The RSC would like to thank Ralph Williams and the University of Michigan for their support in the development of *Cardenio*.

The RSC is grateful for the significant support of its principal funder, Arts Council England, without which our work would not be possible. Around 50 per cent of the RSC's income is self-generated from Box Office sales, sponsorship, donations, enterprise and partnerships with other organisations.

Supported by
**ARTS COUNCIL
ENGLAND**

This production of *Cardenio* was first performed by the
Royal Shakespeare Company in the Swan Theatre,
Stratford-upon-Avon, on 14th April 2011. The cast was as follows:

DUKE RICARDO OF AGUILAR	**Christopher Ettridge**
PEDRO (his elder son)	**Simeon Moore**
FERNANDO (his younger son)	**Alex Hassell**
GERARDO	**Chiké Okonkwo**
DON BERNARDO	**Nicholas Day**
LUSCINDA (his daughter)	**Lucy Briggs-Owen**
DUENNA	**Liz Crowther**
DON CAMILLO	**Christopher Godwin**
CARDENIO (his son)	**Oliver Rix**
DOROTEA	**Pippa Nixon**
MAID	**Matti Houghton**
MASTER SHEPHERD	**Timothy Speyer**
FIRST SHEPHERD	**Michael Grady-Hall**
SECOND SHEPHERD	**Felix Hayes**
PRIEST	**Christopher Chilton**
CITIZEN	**Harry Myers**
NUN	**Maya Barcot**

All other parts played by members of the company.

Directed by	**Gregory Doran**
Designed by	**Niki Turner**
Lighting Designed by	**Tim Mitchell**
Music by	**Paul Englishby**
Sound by	**Martin Slavin**
Movement by	**Michael Ashcroft**
Fights by	**Terry King**
Company Text and Voice work by	**Jacquie Crago**
Assistant Director	**Ben Brynmor**
Music Director	**Bruce O'Neil**
Dramaturg	**Jeanie O'Hare**
Casting by	**Hannah Miller** CDG
Production Manager	**Mark Graham**
Costume Supervisor	**Bill Butler**
Company Manager	**Jondon**
Stage Manager	**Alix Harvey-Thompson**
Deputy Stage Manager	**Jenny Grand**
Assistant Stage Manager	**Mark McGowan**

MUSICIANS

Voice	**Javier Macías**
Guitar	**Luis Carro Barquero**
Guitar	**Nicholas Lee**
Percussion	**James Jones**

This text may differ slightly from the play as performed.

JOIN US

Join us from £18 a year.

Join today and make a difference

The Royal Shakespeare Company is an ensemble. We perform all year round in our Stratford-upon-Avon home, as well as having regular seasons in London, and touring extensively within the UK and overseas for international residencies.

With a range of options from £18 to £10,000 per year, there are many ways to engage with the RSC.

Choose a level that suits you and enjoy a closer connection with us whilst also supporting our work on stage.

Find us online

Sign up for regular email updates at **www.rsc.org.uk/signup**

Join today

Annual RSC Full Membership costs just £40 (or £18 for Associate Membership) and provides you with regular updates on RSC news, advance information and priority booking.

Support us

A charitable donation from £100 a year can offer you the benefits of membership, whilst also allowing you the opportunity to deepen your relationship with the Company through special events, backstage tours and exclusive ticket booking services.

The options include Shakespeare's Circle (from £100), Patrons' Circle (Silver: £1,000, Gold: £5,000) and Artists' Circle (£10,000).

For more information visit **www.rsc.org.uk/joinus** or call the RSC Membership Office on 01789 403 440.

THE ROYAL SHAKESPEARE COMPANY

CARDENIO

Shakespeare's 'Lost Play' Re-imagined

After
Double Falshood; or The Distrest Lovers
by Lewis Theobald (1727)

Apparently revised
from a manuscript in the handwriting of John Downes
and conceivably adapted by Sir William Davenant for
Thomas Betterton from
The History of Cardenio
by Mr Fletcher and Shakespeare (1612)
performed at Court in 1612/13

Which may have been based on an episode in
Don Quixote
by Miguel de Cervantes
which was translated into English
by Thomas Shelton
First published in 1612

And here adapted and directed by Gregory Doran
for the Royal Shakespeare Company
With additional Spanish material supplied by Antonio Álamo
via a literal translation by Duncan Wheeler
and developed in rehearsal by the original cast

Contents

Introduction

Theatre is the most collaborative of the arts; and collaboration
has been the key note of *Cardenio* since William Shakespeare
and his younger colleague John Fletcher decided to write a play
together, based on an episode in the Spanish best-seller, *Don
Quixote* by Miguel de Cervantes Saavedra, first published in
England in 1612, in a translation by Thomas Shelton.

Cardenio somehow avoided inclusion in either the First Folio of
Shakespeare's plays in 1623, or of Humphrey Moseley's
publication of Beaumont and Fletcher's plays in 1647. But
Moseley did register *The History of Cardenio* by Mr Fletcher. &
Shakespeare (sic) for publication in 1653, in the Stationers'
Register. Perhaps Sir William Davenant (who promoted the
rumour that he was Shakespeare's illegitimate child) had a
manuscript of this play, and may have prepared it for
performance by his company after the Restoration, with
Thomas Betterton, the leading tragedian of his time, as
Cardenio himself. Davenant's company had done adaptations of
the two other Shakespeare/Fletcher collaborations we know
about: *The Two Noble Kinsmen* and *All is True (Henry VIII)*; so
why not *Cardenio*?

The prompter to that company, one John Downes, retired in
1706, and it seems a manuscript copy of *Cardenio*, in his
handwriting, fell into the hands of one Lewis Theobald.
Theobald, who had trained in the law, had tried his hand at
everything: classical translation, journalism, poetry, opera
librettos and even a novel, and was scratching a living writing
the new popular pantomimes at the theatre in Lincoln's Inn
Fields. But he finally came to prominence by challenging the
great poet of the Augustan Age, Alexander Pope, for his sloppy
inaccurate edition of Shakespeare. And Theobald's follow-up
move, designed to secure his place in the literary pantheon, was

his adaptation of that *Cardenio* manuscript, which he called *Double Falshood, or The Distrest Lovers*. It was a success. It ran for ten consecutive performances at Drury Lane Theatre.

Back in 2003, when I was directing Fletcher's *The Tamer Tamed*, his sequel to *The Taming of the Shrew*, we got a group of actors together to read Theobald's *Double Falshood*. We all agreed that it had great potential, but that the plotting (particularly at the beginning) was convoluted, and it was missing several scenes. At which point, we put the play aside. However, after re-reading Shelton's 1612 translation of *Don Quixote*, I realised that those missing scenes might be re-imagined from the very same source material that Shakespeare and Fletcher must have used.

In 2007 on a visit to Spain with *The Canterbury Tales*, I was introduced by the Almagro Festival director, Emilio Hernandez, to Antonio Álamo, a writer and the director of the Lope de Vega Theatre in Seville. Antonio is a Cervantes nut, so we inevitably discussed *Cardenio*. He alerted me to what an extraordinary story it is, and made me realise just how much Theobald (who admitted he was adapting it for the tastes and sensibilities of the London audience of his time) had removed: namely, much of the psychological complexity and rigour of the original. We would need to replace *Cardenio*'s 'cojones'!

Further discussion with Spanish colleagues ensued. I travelled to Cordoba to accept a Bellas Artes medal, on behalf of the RSC, from the King of Spain (Laurence Boswell's brilliant Spanish Golden Age Season had visited Madrid, as had my own production of *Coriolanus*: both had emanated from the RSC). In Alicante at a Cervantes/Shakespeare conference organised by Professor Jose Manuel Gonzalez de Sevilla, further discussions took place – and finally a visit to Seville with Antonio Álamo, to understand the significance of the story in Spain. Out of this visit came another draft, which we workshopped with the *Hamlet* company in 2008, and another draft was further developed at an RSC residency in Michigan, under the aegis of Professor Ralph Williams. Here we worked with Hispanic-American actors from the LAByrinth theatre company in New York. So, for example,

Cardenio was played by a Mexican, and Don Bernardo by an actor from Los Angeles, which certainly revealed and rooted the play's Spanish temperament.

Throughout the process, we poured over other seventeenth-century versions of the Cardenio story, by Pichou, by de Castro, by Bouscal, and by Thomas D'Urfey. But in an attempt to provide some sense of integrity to the piece, where extra lines were needed, I tried to limit myself to plundering only those Jacobean plays in which John Fletcher had drawn upon Cervantes.

Cardenio is the first new production in the Swan Theatre, since the RSC's Transformation Project (another collaborative effort if ever there was one). The Swan opened twenty-five years ago with Fletcher and Shakespeare's *The Two Noble Kinsmen*, so it is only fitting that we return with another play they worked on together, although this time the list of writing credits has grown to the length of a Hollywood blockbuster, with Shakespeare, Cervantes, Fletcher, Shelton, Theobald, etc.

Thanks to everyone who collaborated on this project: to Jeanie O'Hare, our company dramaturg, for her eagle eye; to Jeremy Adams, our indefatigable producer, who has nurtured the project throughout; to Ann Bateson our Spanish 'fixer'; to all the actors who worked on the various workshops; to Réjane Collard for arranging various literal translations for us; to Emilio Hernandez, to Antonio Álamo, to Professor Jose Manuel Gonzalez, and to all our Spanish colleagues; to Chris Hickey, who was Head of the British Council in Madrid, for his advice; to Professor Ralph Williams and the folk at Michigan University; to Gordon McMullan who first steered me towards Fletcher; to Professor Brean Hammond who edited the Arden edition of *Double Falshood*; and to Professor Tiffany Stern, who wisely cautioned scepticism.

And finally to Lewis Theobald, for excavating his 'dear relic'.

Gregory Doran
Stratford-upon-Avon
Lady Day, 2011

Characters

DUKE RICARDO OF AGUILAR
PEDRO, *his son*
FERNANDO, *his younger son*
CARDENIO
DON CAMILLO, *his father*
LUSCINDA, *beloved of Cardenio*
DON BERNARDO, *her father*
GERARDO
DOROTEA, *a wealthy farmer's daughter*
DOROTEA'S MAID
A CITIZEN
PRIEST
DUENNA
MASTER OF THE FLOCK
FIRST SHEPHERD
SECOND SHEPHERD
NOVICE, *in the convent*

This text went to press before the end of rehearsals and so may differ slightly from the play as performed.

ACT ONE

Scene One

The Palace of DUKE RICARDO.

Enter the DUKE, DON RICARDO *and* PEDRO.

PEDRO.
My gracious father, this unwonted strain
Visits my heart with sadness.

DUKE.

Why, my son?
Making my death familiar to my tongue
Digs not my grave one jot before the date.
I've worn the garland of my honours long,
And would not leave it withered to thy brow,
But flourishing and green; worthy the man,
Who, with my Dukedoms, heirs my better glories.

PEDRO.
This praise, which is my pride, spreads me with blushes.

DUKE.
Think not that I can flatter thee my Pedro;
Or let the scale of love o'er-poise my judgement.
Like the fair glass of retrospection, thou
Reflect'st the virtues of my early youth;
Making my old blood mend its pace with transport:
While fond Fernando, thy irregular brother,
Sets the large credit of his name at stake,
A truant to my wishes, and his birth.
His taints of wildness hurt our nicer honour,
And call for swift reclaim.

PEDRO.

                              I trust my brother
  Will, by the vantage of his cooler wisdom
  Erewhile redeem the hot escapes of youth,
  And court opinion with a golden conduct.

DUKE.

  Be thou a prophet in that kind suggestion!
  But I, by fears weighing his unweighed course,
  Interpret for the future from the past.
  And strange misgivings, why he hath of late
  By importunity, and strained petition,
  Wrested our leave of absence from the court,
  Awake suspicion. Thou art inward with him;
  And haply, from the bosom'd trust, canst shape
  Some formal cause to qualify my doubts.

PEDRO.

  Why he hath pressed this absence, sir, I know not;
  But that he tells me he would have the means
  To purchase certain horse, that like him well,
  And asks Cardenio, good Camillo's son,
  A youth well tried in noble horsemanship,
  To help him in this latest enterprise.
  This Cardenio he encountered first in France,
  And lovingly commends him to my favour.

DUKE.

  I have upon Fernando's strong request
  Sent for Cardenio to come to court.
  Do thou assay to mould him, my dear son,
  An honest spy upon thy brother's riots.
  Make us acquainted when the youth arrives.

  Exeunt.

Scene Two

The Town of Almodovar.

Enter LUSCINDA *and* CARDENIO.

CARDENIO.
>   Luscinda, love,
> Urge not suspicions of what cannot be;
> You deal unkindly; mis-becomingly,
> I'm loath to say: for all that waits on you,
> Is graced, and graces. – No impediment
> Shall bar my wishes, but such grave delays
> As reason presses patience with; which blunt not,
> But rather whet our loves.

LUSCINDA.
> You purchase at too dear a rate, that puts you
> To woo me and your father too: besides
> As he, perchance, may say, you shall not have me;
> You, who are so obedient, must discharge me
> Out of your fancy; then, Cardenio,
> 'Twill prove my sorrow, meeting such repulse,
> To wear the willow in my prime of youth.

CARDENIO.
> Oh! do not rack me with these ill-placed doubts;
> Nor think, though age has in my father's breast
> Put out love's flame, he therefore has not eyes,
> Or is in judgement blind. You wrong your beauties,
> Venus will frown if you despise her gifts,
> That have a face would make a frozen hermit
> Leap from his cell, and burn his beads to kiss it;
> Eyes, that are nothing but continual births
> Of new desires in those that view their beams.
> You cannot have a cause to doubt.

LUSCINDA.

O, why?
When you that dare not choose without your father
And, where you love, you dare not vouch it; must not,
Though you have eyes, see with 'em; – can I, think you,
Somewhat, perhaps infected by your suit,
Sit down content to say, 'you would, but dare not'?

CARDENIO.

I do not see that fervour in thee now
Which youth and love should kindle. You consent
As 'twere to feed without an appetite. This affection
Is such a feigned one, as will break untouched;
Die frosty, ere it can be thawed; while mine,
Like to a clime beneath Hyperion's eye,
Burns with one constant heat.

LUSCINDA.

My father –

Enter DON BERNARDO.

DON BERNARDO.

What, Cardenio, in public? This wooing is too urgent. Is
your father yet moved in the suit, who must be the prime
unfolder of this business?

CARDENIO.

I have not yet, indeed at full possessed
My father, whom it is my service follows;
But only that I have a wife in chase.

DON BERNARDO.

Chase! – Let chase alone: no matter for that. – You may halt
after her, whom you profess to pursue, and catch her too;
marry, not unless your father let you slip. – Briefly, I desire
you (for she tells me, my instructions shall be both eyes and
feet to her); no farther to insist in your requiring, till, as I
have formerly said, Camillo make known to me, that his
good liking goes along with us: which once but breathed, all
is done; till when the business has no life, and cannot find a
beginning.

CARDENIO.

Sir, I will know his mind, e'er I taste sleep;
At morn, you shall be learn'd in his desire
I take my leave. – O virtuous Luscinda,
Repose, sweet as thy beauties, seal thy eyes;
Once more, adieu. Remember and be faithful.

Exit CARDENIO.

DON BERNARDO.

His father is as unsettled as he is wayward in his
disposition. If I thought young Cardenio's temper were not
mended by the metal of his mother, I should be something
crazy in giving my consent to this match: and, to tell you
true, if my eyes might be the directors to your mind, I could
in this town look upon twenty men of more delicate choice.
I speak not this altogether to unbend your affections to him:
but the meaning of what I say is that you set such price upon
yourself to him, as many, and much his betters, would buy
you at (and reckon those virtues in you at the rate of their
scarcity); to which if he come not up, you remain for a
better mart.

LUSCINDA.

My obedience, sir, is chained to your advice.

DON BERNARDO.

'Tis well said and wisely. I fear your lover is a little folly-
tainted; which, shortly after it proves so, you will repent.

LUSCINDA.

Sir, I confess, I approve him of all the men I know; but that
approbation is nothing, till seasoned by your consent.

DON BERNARDO.

We shall hear soon what his father will do, and so proceed
accordingly. I have no great heart to the business, neither
will I with any violence oppose it: but leave it to that power
which rules in these conjunctions, and there's an end. Come,
haste we homeward, girl.

Exeunt.

Scene Three

Enter DON CAMILLO *with a letter.*

DON CAMILLO.

How comes the Duke to take such notice of my son, that he must needs have him in the court, and I must send him upon the view of this letter?

– Horsemanship! What horsemanship has Cardenio? I think he can no more but gallop a hackney, unless he practised riding in France. It may be he did so; for he was there a good continuance. But I have not heard him speak much of his horsemanship. That's no matter: if he be not a good horseman, all's one in such a case, he must bear. Princes are absolute; they may do what they will in any thing, save what they cannot do.

Enter CARDENIO.

O, come on, sir; read this paper: the Duke Ricardo is disposed to favour you.

CARDENIO *tries to speak but his father interrupts.*

No more ado, but read it: it must not be answered by my hand, nor yours, but in gross, by your person; your sole person. Read aloud.

CARDENIO.

Please you, to let me first o'er look it, sir.

DON CAMILLO.

I was this other day in a spleen against your new suits: I do now think some fate was the tailor that hath fitted them: for, this hour, they are for the Palace of the Duke.

CARDENIO.

Hah! To court?

DON CAMILLO.

Your father's house is too dusty. Duke Ricardo as I think you know, is a grandee of Spain, his Dukedom in the best part of all Andalusia.

CARDENIO (*aside*).

Which is the better, to serve a mistress, or a Duke? I am sued to be his slave, and I sue to be Luscinda's.

DON CAMILLO.

You shall find your horsemanship much praised there; are you so good a horseman?

CARDENIO.

I have been e'er now commended for my seat, or mocked.

DON CAMILLO.

Take one commendation with another, every third's a mock. Affect not therefore to be praised. Here's a deal of command and entreaty mixed; there's no denying; you must go, peremptorily he enforces that.

CARDENIO (*aside*).

What fortune so' ever my going shall encounter, cannot be good fortune; what I part withal unseasons any other goodness.

DON CAMILLO.

You must needs go; he rather conjures, than importunes.

CARDENIO (*aside*).

No moving of my love suit to him now.

DON CAMILLO.

Great fortunes have grown out of less grounds.

CARDENIO (*aside*).

What may her father think of me, who expects to be solicited this very night?

DON CAMILLO.

Those scattered pieces of virtue, which are in him, the court will solder together, varnish, and rectify.

CARDENIO (*aside*).
  He will surely think I deal too slightly, or unmannerly, or
  foolishly, indeed; nay dishonestly; to bear him in hand with
  my father's consent, who yet hath not been touched with so
  much as a request to it.

DON CAMILLO.
  Well, sir, have you read it over?

CARDENIO.
  Yes, sir.

DON CAMILLO.
  And considered it?

CARDENIO.
  As I can.

DON CAMILLO.
  If you can be courted by good fortune, you must go.

CARDENIO.
  So it please you, sir.

DON CAMILLO.
  By any means, and tomorrow: is it not there the limits of his
  request?

CARDENIO.
  It is, sir.

DON CAMILLO.
  Thou must straight depart to accomplish the Duke's desire;
  and omit not to render Almighty God thanks, which doth
  thus open the way by which thou mayest attain, in fine, to
  that which I know thou dost merit.

CARDENIO.
  Father...

DON CAMILLO.
  I must bethink me of some necessaries, without which you
  might be unfurnished: and my supplies shall at all
  convenience follow you. Come to my closet by and by; I
  would there speak with you.

Exit DON CAMILLO.

CARDENIO.
Address me to the Duke Ricardo's court,
That I might be companion to his son?
I must perforce obey my father's will.
But straight to my Luscinda I'll recount
What here has passed, likewise her father
Entreating him overslip a day or two,
Defer bestowing my sweet love elsewhere
Until we understand the Duke's high will.

LUSCINDA *appears at the grilled window.*

See, how her beauty doth enrich the place!
O, add the music of thy charming tongue,
Sweet as the lark that wakens up the morn,
And make me think it paradise indeed.

LUSCINDA.
What says your father?

CARDENIO.
I have not moved him yet.

LUSCINDA.
                              Then do not so.

CARDENIO.
Not move him? Was it not your own command,
That his consent should ratify our loves?

LUSCINDA.
Perhaps, it was: But now I have changed my mind.

CARDENIO.
Be patient, sweet.

LUSCINDA.
Patient! What else? My flames are in the flint.
Haply, to lose a husband I may weep;
Never to get one: when I cry bondage,
Let freedom quit me.

CARDENIO.
                        From what a spirit comes this?
I now perceive too plain, you care not for me.
Duke, I obey thy summons, be its tenour
Whate'er it will: if war, I come thy soldier:
Or if to waste my silken hours at court,
The slave of fashion, I with willing soul
Embrace the lazy banishment for life;
Since Luscinda has pronounced my doom.

LUSCINDA.
What do you mean? Why talk you of the Duke?
Wherefore of war, or court, or banishment?

CARDENIO (*showing her the* DUKE's *letter*).
How this new note is grown of me I know not:
But the Duke writes for me. Coming to move
My father in our bus'ness, I did find him
Reading this letter; whose contents require
My instant service, and repair to court.

LUSCINDA.
Now I perceive the birth of these delays;
Why Luscinda was not worth your suit.
Repair to Court? Ay, there you shall perhaps,
(Rather, past doubt) behold some choicer beauty
Rich in her charms, trained to the arts of soothing,
Shall prompt you to a spirit of hardiness,
To say, 'So please you, Father, I have chosen
This mistress of my own.'

CARDENIO.
                        Still you mistake me:
Ever your servant I profess myself;
And will not blot me with a change, for all
That sea and land inherit.

LUSCINDA.
                        But when go you?

CARDENIO.

    Tomorrow, love, so runs the Duke's command;
    Stinting our farewell kisses, cutting off
    The forms of parting, and the interchange
    Of thousand precious vows, with haste too rude.
    Lovers have things of moment to debate,
    More than a prince, or dreaming statesman know:
    Such ceremonies wait on Cupid's throne.
    Why heaved that sigh?

LUSCINDA.

                  O Cardenio, let me whisper
    What, but for parting, I would blush to tell thee:
    My heart beats thick with fears, lest the gay scene,
    The splendours of a court, should from thy breast
    Banish my image, kill my interest in thee,
    And I will be left the scoff of maids, to drop
    A widow's tear for thy departed faith.

CARDENIO.

    O, let assurance, strong as words can bind,
    Tell thy pleased soul, I will be wondrous faithful;
    As the sun to its race of light,
    As shade to darkness, as desire to beauty:
    As when I swerve, let wretchedness o'ertake me,
    Great as e'er falsehood met, or change can merit.

LUSCINDA.

    Enough, I'm satisfied: and will remain
    Yours, with a firm and untired constancy.
    Make not your absence long: old men are wavering;
    And swayed by interest more than promise given.
    Should some other offer start, when you're away,
    I may be pressed to something, which must put
    My faith, or my obedience, to the rack.

CARDENIO.

    Fear not, but I with swiftest wing of time
    Will labour my return.

    Exits.

Scene Four

A village in Andalusia. Night.

Enter FERNANDO, GERARDO *and servants with lights.*

FERNANDO.
Bear the lights close: – where is the music, sirs?

GERARDO.
Coming, my lord.

FERNANDO.
Let 'em not come too near. This maid,
For whom my sighs ride on the night's chill vapour,
Is born most humbly, though she be as fair
As nature's richest mould and skill can make her,
Mended with strong imagination.
But what of that? Th'obscureness of her birth
Cannot eclipse the lustre of her eyes,
Which make her all one light. Strike up, my masters;
But touch the strings with a religious softness;
Teach sound to languish thro' the night's dull ear,
Till melancholy start from her lazy couch
And carelessness grow convert to attention.

Music plays.

She drives me into wonder. When I sometimes
Hear her discourse, the court, whereof report
And guess alone inform her, she will rave at,
As if she there seven reigns had slandered time.
Then, when she reasons on her country state,
Health, virtue, plainness, and simplicity,
On beauties true in title, scorning art,
Freedom as well to do, as think what's good;
My heart grows sick of birth and empty rank

And I become a villager in wish.
Play on; – she sleeps too sound: – be still and vanish:
A gleam of day breaks sudden from her window:
O taper graced by that midnight hand!

DOROTEA *appears above at the window.*

DOROTEA.
Who is't that woos at this late hour? What are you?

FERNANDO.
One who for your dear sake watches the starless night!

DOROTEA.
My Lord Fernando, or my ear deceives me.
You've had my answer and 'tis more than strange
You'll combat these repulses. Good my lord,
Be friend to your own health, and give me leave,
Securing my poor fame, nothing to pity
What pangs you swear you suffer. 'Tis impossible
To plant your choice affections in my shade,
At least, for them to grow there.

FERNANDO.

                    Why, Dorotea.

DOROTEA.
Alas! Sir, there are reasons numberless,
To bar your aims. Be warned to hours more wholesome;
For these you watch in vain. I have read stories
(I fear, too true ones); how young lords like you,
Have thus besung mean windows, rhymed their sufferings
Even to the abuse of things divine, set up
Plain girls, like me, the idols of their worship,
Then left them to bewail their easy faith,
And stand the world's contempt.

FERNANDO.

                    Your memory,
Too faithful to the wrongs of few lost maids,
Makes fear too general.

DOROTEA.

Let us be homely,
And let us too be chaste, doing you lords no wrong;
But crediting your oaths with such a spirit,
As you profess them, so no party trusted
Shall make a loosing bargain. Home, my lord,
What you can say is most unseasonable; what sing
Most absonant and harsh; nay, your perfume,
Which I smell hither, cheers not my sense
Like our field violet's breath.

FERNANDO.

Why this dismission
Does more invite my staying.

DOROTEA.

Men of your temper
Make everything their bramble. But I wrong
That which I am preserving, my maid's name,
To hold so long discourse. Your virtues guide you
T'effect some nobler purpose!

Exit DOROTEA.

FERNANDO.

Stay, bright maid!
Come back, and leave me with a fairer hope.
She's gone, no matter I will bribe her woman,
And soon shall gain admittance. –
Who am I that am thus contemned?
The second son of a prince? Yes, well, what then?
Why your great birth forbids you to descend
To a low alliance: – hers is the selfsame stuff,
Whereof we dukes are made: but clay more pure!
And take away my title, which is but acquired
Not by myself, but thrown by fortune on me,
Or by the merit of some ancestor
Of singular quality, she doth inherit
Deserts t'outweigh me. I must stoop to gain her;
Throw all my gay caparisons aside

And turn my proud additions out of service,
Rather than keep them to become my masters.
The dignities we wear, are gifts of pride;
And laugh'd at by the wise, as mere outside.

Exits.

Scene Five

The Ducal Palace.

Enter PEDRO *and* CARDENIO.

PEDRO.
In this brief interval of time since you
Arrived with us in court, Cardenio,
The Duke hath shown such tokens of his love,
That all men wonder at it.

CARDENIO.
                          Gracious Lord,
So friendly has my entertainment been,
I blush at my too poor unworthiness.

PEDRO.
And he that most rejoices at your stay,
My brother Don Fernando, holds you so
Entirely in his love, so dear in his esteem
That envy 'gins to exercise her old
Accustomed function…

CARDENIO.
                          I will labour, sir, to…

PEDRO.
The great Duke burns with a desire to know
The reason for his absences from court,
And would receive it as a favour, sir

Which you may grant, and must not be denied,
T'acquaint him with as much as may be known.

CARDENIO.

I see the mark you shoot at, sir, but dare...

PEDRO.

                    The Duke
Commands my present ear. I commend you
And study your advancement with that care
As I would do a brother's. Here he comes.

Enter FERNANDO *as from riding.*

FERNANDO.

This breaking of horses a little stirs the blood.
The English with their slothful industry
Aim for the most part for no greater skill
Than riding of a ridden perfect horse.
But a true rider breaks the horse himself,
And brings his mare from utter ignorance
To the bravest skill can ever be desired.

PEDRO.

Good morrow, brother, you are early up.

FERNANDO.

From this he finds a twofold pleasure, sir,
The excellent contentment of his mind,
And body's healthful recreation too.

PEDRO.

I'll leave you for this time. Good brother mine.

FERNANDO.

Behold this fiery gallant, brother, he
Hath no fellow for noble horsemanship.
Why, you may see him grow into his seat
And to such wondrous doings bring his horse
As he had been incorpsed with the beast.
Why, Perseus did not know his seat like him;
The Parthian that rides swift without the rein,
Matched not his grace and firmness, eh my lord?

Exit PEDRO.

> Among the gifts which in his bounty Jove
> Bestows upon me with a liberal hand,
> I find myself most highly bound to him
> For having given such a friend as thou.

CARDENIO.

> And I with all solicitude and care
> Regard the amity you've shown to me,
> As precious to my heart.

FERNANDO.

> > > > Cardenio.
> Now tell me further of this damosel,
> Thy dear Luscinda whom thou missest so,
> And whom thou told'st me of so very late.
> I long to hear thy secret treasury.

CARDENIO.

> How love delights to chatter of its self.
> If in this world there is a Heaven, lord,
> Wherein love places all that I desire
> It is in her; so great her beauty is.
> Luscinda, I have loved and honoured so
> Almost from infancy and she likewise
> Affected me with all th'integrity
> Which her young years allowed. Our age increased
> And so did our affection, in such sort
> That it seemed fit, that her good father should
> Deny me further entrance of his house...

FERNANDO.

> As Thisbe's father did to Pyramus.

CARDENIO.

> Which weighty hindr'nce only served to add
> Desire to desire, flame to flame.
> Although this set a silence to our tongues,
> Yet could it not impose it to our pens,
> Which oft express (in deepest terms, my lord),
> The hidden secrets of our very souls.

How many letters have I written her
How many ditties and amorous verses too
Have I composed wherein my soul declared
Published my passion.

FERNANDO.

The familiarity
I have with thee now passes far beyond
The limits favour bears, and turns to love
Therefore, 'tis not of horses only that I crave
Your sound advice, my dear Cardenio.
And so as there's no secrecy 'mong friends,
I must reveal unto thee all my thoughts,
But chiefly one of love, my sweetest friend.
I have a mistress too, if thou wouldst hear.

CARDENIO.

Gladly, my lord.

FERNANDO.

Then thus Cardenio.
I am enamoured on a farmer's daughter,
That is my father's vassal, it falls out,
And marvellously rich her parents are.
She is so modest and so beautiful,
As never one that knew her can decide
In which of her perfections she excels.
And those good parts of this young country maid
Have wrought in my desire this resolve:
That I might conquer her integrity,
By promising to marry her anon,
For otherwise I strive against the stream.

CARDENIO.

What is her name?

FERNANDO.

Her name is Dorotea.

CARDENIO.

And your father, the Duke, Don Ricardo,
Does he know aught of this? Does he approve?

Bound by the friendship that I have for you,
Which equals that you say you have for me,
I must dissuade you from your purpose, sir,
And thwart it till the Duke approves the match.

FERNANDO.
Pray you choose some other theme, Cardenio.
Is the Neopolitan in a fit plight to run?

CARDENIO.
Give me leave
To argue with you, and the fondness of
Affection struck blind, with justice hear me:
And do not fling your life into the furnace
Of your father's anger.

FERNANDO.
A mare must first receive you on her back,
Which only may with patience be achieved.

CARDENIO.
Love for the most part is not love but lust,
Which ever seeks delight as his last end.
So soon as it obtains the same it dies,
Decayeth and makes forcible retire.

FERNANDO.
She'll gain the knowledge of her master's will
With cheerful helps, and careful cherishings.

Enter GERARDO.

GERARDO.
The Duke with all good speed expects you, sir.

CARDENIO.
Maids are not toys to play with, good my lord.

FERNANDO.
Love! Is there such a word in any language
Carries honest sense? Come, Cardenio.

Exeunt.

Scene Six

DOROTEA*'s chamber. Night.*

It is quiet. Music plays in the distance.

DOROTEA.
Is there a Fiesta in the square tonight?

MAID.
No man can sleep for music.

DOROTEA.
                    What again?
Who pays for all these revels, and these sports?
Hast thou made safe the doors, my girl, pray see?

MAID.
Please you, madam, I'm not so certain, now.

The MAID *leaves.* FERNANDO *enters.*

DOROTEA.
Why Lord Fernando? Pray what do you here?

FERNANDO.
What do I here? Why, pray! Do you not see?
Or love of understanding quite is void:
Or he abounds in cruelty. The pain,
The dire torments love makes me sustain
My heart can scarce abide without your help.

DOROTEA.
If I were now between a lion's paws
And were made certain sure of liberty
If only I'd forsake my honour here,
'Twould prove all as impossible for me
As for the lion to give his essence o'er.
Then even as you have engirt me round
So likewise have I binded fast my mind

With virtuous and forcible desires
(All which are wholly different from yours),
As you shall find if force you seek to use.

FERNANDO.

Pray, who ordains this ache I worship.

DOROTEA.

I am your vassal, not your slave, my lord;
Nor ought the nobleness of your high blood
Have power to stain the humbleness of mine.
I do esteem myself (though but a girl,
A farmer's daughter, but a country wench),
As much as you yourself, though noble born.

FERNANDO.

Such evil in such goodness will not fit.

DOROTEA.

With me your violence cannot prevail,
Your wealth gain grace, your words have power to cheat
Nor yet your sighs and tears have power to move;
Yet if these properties reside in him
Whom it shall please my parents to bestow
On me for spouse, I will subject my will
To his, nor shall it vary, not one jot.

So that if I remain with honour there,
Although I rested void of more delights,
Yet would I willingly bestow on him,
That which you labour so much to obtain.

I say this to divert your straying thought
From ever thinking that he may obtain
But aught of me who's not my lawful spouse.

FERNANDO.

If that the let only consists therein,
Behold my Dorotea, I give thee here
My hand to be but thine, and thine alone;
And let bright Heaven, from whom naught is concealed,
And this Our Lady's holy image here
Be witness of this truth.

DOROTEA.

> I beg you, lord, to look well what you do.
> Your father will be angry when he sees
> You married to a vassal base as I.

> Take heed my beauty blind you not, my lord,
> 'Tis not sufficient to excuse this fault:
> And if you mean to do me any good
> I conjure you, by any love you bear,
> To let my fortunes roll in their own sphere,
> According as my quality may reach;
> For such unequal matches ne'er please long,
> Nor long preserve the pleasure they begin.

FERNANDO.

> My Dorotea you are not the first
> By marriage to ascend from low degree;
> Nor I am not the first to make a choice
> Unequal to the greatness of my state.
> And since herein no new worlds we create
> Embrace this honour. Fortune crowns thy fate.
> I'll be your husband in the eyes of God.

> But if disdainfully you now repulse
> My ardent suit, and spurn my offer back,
> I may forget I am a nobleman,
> And stain with violence this holy pact.

> What reasons, Dorotea, might there be
> Sufficient to persuade your father's mind
> A gentleman of such estate as I
> Would enter in your room without consent?

DOROTEA.

> I'll call my waiting maid, that she on earth
> Might company keep with this celestial witness.
> Without there ho!

The MAID *enters.*

FERNANDO (*to* DOROTEA).

> Oh, do not doubt me. I have heard men say
> Love sometime flies and other times it walks;

With this love runs, with that love slowly goes;
Inflames this one and leaves the next key-cold.
Some it wounds, some others yet it kills;
Begins in a moment and in a moment dies.
In the morning, lays siege to a fortress
And by night-time has forced it to yield.
There is no power able to resist.
Then abide by what love has determined.

FERNANDO *gives her a ring.*

My Dorotea, these oaths again I swear,
And call the saints in clouds to witness it,
And wish a thousand maledictions light
Upon my head if I accomplish not
My promises of faithfulness to thee.

The ceremony has taken place.

The Fiesta continues outside.

End of Act One.

ACT TWO

Scene One

*The village. Early hours of the morning. The Fiesta is still
going on. A drunken dance, wild and savage.* FERNANDO
enters from the house. CARDENIO, *who has been watching the
Fiesta, catches sight of him.*

FERNANDO.
Ha! Is it come to this? Oh, the Devil, the Devil, the Devil!
Where were the eyes, the voice, the various charms,
Each beauteous particle, each nameless grace,
Parents of glowing love? All these in her,
It seems, were not: but a disease in me
That fancied graces in her. – Soft! mine honour
Begins to sicken in this black reflection.

CARDENIO.
Why, there he is. My lord? He hears me not.
Why does he stalk so, and goggle with his eyes?
Sure, his brains will boil over...

FERNANDO.

Shame, shame, upon it!

CARDENIO.
Now the storm grows high. Is he touched?

FERNANDO.
Hold, let me be severe to myself, but not unjust. Was it rape
then? No, her shrieks, her exclamations then had drove me
from her. True, she did consent; as true she did resist, but
still in silence all. And is the man yet born, who would not
risk the guilt to meet the joy? The guilt! That's true – but
then the danger; the tears, the clamours of the ruined maid,
pursuing me to court. That, that I fear, will (as it already does
my conscience) something shatter my honour.

CARDENIO.
Too much heat. My lord?

FERNANDO.
What Cardenio, here?
My guilt conjures him hither! Cardenio!
Thou tak'st me in an ill planet, my friend.
When the stars flow with misfortune,
Precipitately falling from above,
No earthly force, nor human industry
Can withhold or prevent their destruction.

CARDENIO.
Come, go we homeward, sir. 'Tis very late.

FERNANDO.
I am now fully sensible of running
Into a violent lethargy, whose deadliness
Locks up all reason. I see my folly.
My rage hath poured upon my reasoning
Clouds of error. I never shall henceforth
Remember my past happiness. I fear
Continual night will overshadow me.

CARDENIO.
These clouds may be dispersed, and morning come.

FERNANDO.
'Love for the most part is not love but lust.'

CARDENIO.
Sir?
In adversity, true school of friendship,
We learn those principles which do confirm
Us friends, never to be forgotten, sir.

They embrace.

FERNANDO.
You seem to me, Cardenio, like the sun
And from my deep and ill-perturbed streams
You rise, like morning after darkling dreams.
My tried true friend. Tomorrow, I intend

That we should ride unto Almodovar,
There we may view and cheapen certain horse.

CARDENIO.
To Almodovar? My native dwelling place.

FERNANDO.
For there, they say the best are to be found.

CARDENIO.
'Tis famed for breeding horses, sir, the best
In all the world. But will the Duke, your father
Not require your presence in the court?

FERNANDO.
Ho, Gerardo!

CARDENIO (*aside*).
O, opportunity so fairly offered,
That I might see Luscinda once again...

FERNANDO.
If ever any had a faithful friend,
I am that man, and I may glory in it.

Exeunt.

Scene Two

Enter DOROTEA.

DOROTEA.
Whom shall I look upon without a blush?
There's not a maid whose eye with virgin gaze
Pierces not my guilt. What will't avail me
To say I was not willing;
Nothing; but that I publish my dishonour,
And wound my fame anew. – O misery,
To seem to all one's neighbours rich, yet know
One's self necessitous and wretched.

Enter MAID, *and afterwards* GERARDO *with a letter.*

MAID.
Madam, here's Gerardo, he brings a letter to you.

DOROTEA.
A letter to me! How I tremble now!
Your lord's for court, good Gerardo, is he not?

GERARDO.
Not so, lady.

DOROTEA.
O my presaging heart! When goes he then?

GERARDO.
His business now steers him some other course.

DOROTEA.
Whither I pray you? How my fears torment me!

GERARDO.
Some two months' progress.

DOROTEA.
                          Whither, whither, sir?
I do beseech you? Good Heavens, I lose all patience.
Did he deliberate this? Or was the business
But then conceived when it was born?

GERARDO.
Lady, I know not that; nor is it in the command I have to
await your answer. For the perusing the letter I commend
you to your leisure.

Exit GERARDO.

DOROTEA.
To hearts like mine, suspense is misery.
Wax, render up thy trust: be the contents
Prosp'rous or fatal they are all my due.

(Reads.) *'Our prudence should now teach us to forget, what
our indiscretion has committed, I have already made one
step towards this wisdom, by prevailing on myself to bid you
farewell.'*

O, O, bitten and flung away!
O, wretched and betrayed! Lost Dorotea!
Heart-wounded with a thousand perjured vows,
Poisoned with studied language and bequeathed
To desperation. I am now become
The tomb of my own honour: a dark mansion
For death alone to dwell in. I invite thee,
Consuming desolation, to this temple
Now fit to be thy spoil; the ruined fabric
Which cannot be repaired, at once o'erthow.

What must I do? – But that's not worth my thought:
I will commend to hazard all the time
That I shall spend hereafter: farewell my father,
Whom I'll no more offend: and men, adieu,
Whom I'll no more believe: and maids, adieu,
Whom I'll no longer shame. The way I go,
As yet I know not. Sorrow be my guide.

Exit DOROTEA.

Scene Three

The street. DON BERNARDO*'s house.*

Enter CARDENIO *and* FERNANDO.

CARDENIO.
Since you desire to see my native town,
And as the laws of amity forbid
To keep a treasure hidden from a friend
Permit me show to you the lady whom
I told you of, my lord. This is her house,
And this the strict and rigorous iron grate
Through which we're wont to parley night by night.
We may by luck see her by candlelight.
O, but here she comes!

LUSCINDA *veiled, with her father,* DON BERNARDO, *and
the* DUENNA *walk by as in procession from evensong.*
CARDENIO *hides.* LUSCINDA *drops her missal which*
FERNANDO *moves forward to pick up for her. Her veil
drops, and* FERNANDO *sees her face. The procession
continues into the house.*

FERNANDO.
 Her veil dropped like a cloud from the sun.
 An angel this, young as the morning,
 Her blushes staining his. Defend me,
 Honest thoughts, I shall grow wild else.
 What eyes are there? What little heavens
 To stir men's contemplations! What a paradise
 Runs through each part she has. Good blood be temperate.
 I must look off: too excellent an object
 Confounds the sense that sees it.

CARDENIO (*coming forward*).
 There is a woman, sir, there is a woman.

FERNANDO.
 Why dost thou wait?

CARDENIO.
 Luscinda's father, sir. Saw you not him?
 And therein lies the difficulty.
 He protracts our marriage, demanding that
 My father should first ask him;
 The which I dare not mention to my dad,
 Fearing lest he won't consent thereto.

FERNANDO.
 I will speak to her father. I venture
 If I vouch for thee, he will not say thee nay.
 And now as one good turn deserves another:
 Beseech you go to court and there ensure
 These six fine horses which we here have seen,
 And which thou hast with diligence checked o'er,
 Are mine, or rather ours. Of all the six,
 The courser, or the jennet or the Turk,

Pick out the one that best doth please thee there.
I will this day write to my elder brother,
That he shall give thee gold to cover them.
Set off tomorrow. Now, adieu, and bid
Farewell to your Luscinda. Explain to her.
I will take care of everything.

CARDENIO.

                    Luscinda,
My love, Luscinda!

LUSCINDA *appears at the grill.*

FERNANDO.

                    Men say gold does all,
Engages all, works through all dangers.
Now I say beauty can do more. The King's Exchequer
Nor all his wealthy Indies, could not draw me
Through half those miseries this piece of pleasure
Might make me leap into. Fair Luscinda!
She reigns confessed the tyrant queen of my
Revolted heart, and Dorotea seems
A brief usurper there. Cardenio
Is shortly by my arts removed – O friendship,
How wilt thou answer that? Oh, that a man
Could reason down this fever of the blood,
Or soothe with words the tumult in his heart!
Then Cardenio, I might be, indeed thy friend.
They only should condemn me, who are born
Devoid of passion, or have never proved
The fierce disputes 'twixt virtue and desire.
While they (and there are some), who have like me
The loose escapes of youthful nature known
Must wink at mine, indulgent to their own.

Exit FERNANDO.

CARDENIO.

And in my absence, my sweet Luscinda,
My noble friend and now my honoured guest
The Lord Fernando, will in my behalf
Hang at thy father's ear and with kind hints

Poured from a friendly tongue, secure my claim;
And play the lover for thy absent Cardenio.

LUSCINDA.
Is there no instance of a friend turned false?
Take heed of that; no love by proxy, Cardenio.
My father...

Exit LUSCINDA.

CARDENIO.
When the stars flow with misfortune,
No earthly force can prevent their destruction.

Exit CARDENIO.

Scene Four

Court.

Enter DUKE, *and* PEDRO *with a letter from* FERNANDO.

PEDRO.
I have his letters of a modern date
Wherein he doth solicit the return of gold
To purchase horses in Almodovar.

DUKE.
More horses? Sure, he has a stable full.

PEDRO.
'Twould seem my brother thinks not so, my lord.
He sends Cardenio, his bosom friend
Whom I now with the growing hour expect.
Wishing I would detain him some few days
To know the value of his well-placed trust.

Fernando, my brother,
Into what dangers are you coursing now?

Exeunt.

Scene Five

Before DON BERNARDO*'s house.*

Enter FERNANDO.

FERNANDO.
> How can it be that with my honour safe
> I should pursue Luscinda for my wife?
> That were accumulating injuries
> To Dorotea first and now Cardenio;
> To her a perjured wretch, to him perfidious;
> And to myself in strongest terms accused
> Of murthering honour wilfully, without which
> My dog's the creature of the nobler kind.
> But pleasure is too strong for reason's curb
> And conscience sinks o'erpowered with beauty's sweets.
> Come Luscinda, authoress of my crime,
> Appear and vindicate thy empire here;
> Aid me to drive this lingering honour hence
> And I am wholly thine.

> *Enter* DON BERNARDO *and* LUSCINDA.

DON BERNARDO.
> Fie my good lord; why would you wait without?
> If you suspect your welcome, I have brought
> My Luscinda to assure you of it.

FERNANDO (*salutes* LUSCINDA).
> O kiss, sweet as the odours of the spring,
> But cold as dews that fall on morning flowers!
> Say Luscinda has your father conquered?
> Shall duty then at last obtain the prize,
> Which you refused to love? And shall Fernando
> Owe all his happiness to good Bernardo?
> Ah! no; I read my ruin in your eyes:

That sorrow, louder than a thousand tongues
Pronounces my despair.

DON BERNARDO.
                    Come, Luscinda,
You are not ignorant, this noble lord,
(Whom but to name restores my failing age)
Has with a lover's eye beheld your beauty
Through which his heart speaks more than language can;
It offers joy and happiness to you
And honour to our house. Imagine then
The birth and qualities of him that loves you;
Which when you know, you cannot rate too dear.

LUSCINDA.
My father, on my knees I do beseech you,
To pause one moment on your daughter's ruin.
I vow, my heart e'en bleeds, but I must thank you
For your past tenderness; and yet distrust
That which is yet to come. Consider, sir,
Whoe'er's the occasion of another's fault,
Cannot himself be innocent. O, give not
The censuring world the occasion to reproach
Your harsh commands; or to my charge lay that
Which most I fear, the fault of disobedience.

DON BERNARDO.
Prithee, fear neither the one nor the other: I tell thee, girl,
there's more fear than danger. For my own part, as soon as
thou art married to this noble lord my fears will be over.

LUSCINDA.
Sir, I should be the vainest of my sex,
Not to esteem myself unworthy far
Of this high honour. Once there was a time
When to have heard my Lord Fernando's vows
Might have subdued my unexperienced heart,
And made me wholly his – but that's now past:
And my firm-plighted faith by your consent
Was long since given to Cardenio.

DON BERNARDO.

Why then, by thy consent, e'en take it back again. Thou, like
a simple wench, has given thy affections to a fellow that
does not care a farthing for them. One that has left thee for a
jaunt to court; as who should say, 'I'll get a place there now,
'tis time enough to marry when I'm turned out of it.'

FERNANDO.

So, surely it should seem, most lovely maid,
Cardenio alas feels nothing of my passion:
His love is but the amusement of an hour,
A short relief from business, or ambition,
The sport of youth, and fashion of the age.
O! had he known the hopes, the doubts, the ardours
Or half the fond varieties of passion
That play the tyrant with my tortured soul;
He had not left thee to pursue his fortune;
To practice cringes in a slavish circle,
And barter real bliss for unsure honour.

LUSCINDA.

Oh, the opposing wind,
Shouldering the tide, makes here a fearful billow:
I needs must perish in it. – Oh, my Lord,
Is it then possible, you can forget
What's due to your great name and princely birth,
To friendship's holy law, to faith reposed,
To truth, to honour, and injured Cardenio?
O think, my lord, how much Cardenio loves you;
Recall his services, his well-tried faith;
Think too this very hour where'er he be,
Your favour is the envy of the court,
And secret triumph of his grateful heart.
Poor Cardenio, how securely thou depend'st
Upon the faith and honour of thy master;
Mistaken youth! This very hour he robs thee
Of all thy heart holds dear. – 'Tis so Fernando
Repays the merits of unhappy Cardenio.

She weeps.

FERNANDO (*aside*).
>My slumbering honour catches the alarm.
>I was to blame to parley with her thus:
>Sh'as shown me to myself. It troubles me.

DON BERNARDO.
>Mad, mad, stark mad by this light.

LUSCINDA.
>I but begin to be so. I conjure you
>By all the tender interests of nature
>By the chaste love 'twixt you, and my dear mother
>(O holy Heav'n, that she were living now!)
>Forgive and pity me. Oh, sir, remember
>I've heard my mother say a thousand times
>Her father would have forced her virgin choice;
>But when the conflict was 'twixt love and duty
>Which should be first obeyed, my mother quickly
>Paid up her vows to love, and married you.
>You thought this well, and she was praised for this;
>For this her name was honoured; disobedience
>Was ne'er imputed to her, her firm love
>Conquered whate'er opposed it, and she prospered
>Long time your wife. My case is now the same;
>You are the father, which you then condemned;
>I what my mother was, but not so happy. –

DON BERNARDO.
>Go to, you are a fool. No doubt, you have old stories enough
>to undo you. – What you can't throw yourself away, but by
>precedent, ha? – You will needs be married to one that will
>none of you? You will be happy nobody's way but your own
>forsooth? But d'ye mark me, spare your tongue for the future
>(and that's using you hardly too, to bid you spare what you
>have a great deal too much of); go, go your ways, and d'ye
>hear? Get ready within these two days to be married to a
>husband you don't deserve; – do it or by my dead father's
>soul you are no acquaintance of mine.

FERNANDO.
>She weeps: be gentler to her, good Bernardo.

LUSCINDA.

> Then woe the day. – I'm circled round with fire;
> No way for my escape but through the flames.
> Oh, can I e'er resolve to live without
> A father's blessing, or abandon Cardenio?
> With other maids, the choice were not so hard;
> Int'rest, that rules the world, has made at last
> A merchandise of hearts; and virgins now
> Choose as they're bid, and wed without esteem.
> But nobler springs shall my affections move;
> Nor own a master but the one I love.

> *Exit* LUSCINDA.

DON BERNARDO.

> Go thy ways contradiction – follow her, my lord; follow her
> in the very heat. This obstinacy must be combated by
> importunity as obstinate.

> *Exit* FERNANDO *after her.*

> The girl says right: her mother was just such another. I
> remember, two of us courted her at the same time. She loved
> neither of us, but she chose me purely to spite that surly old
> blockhead my father-in-law.

> *Enter* DON CAMILLO.

> Who comes here, Camillo? Now the refusing part will lie on
> my side –

DON CAMILLO.

> My worthy neighbour, I am much in fortune's favour to find
> you thus alone. I have a suit to you.

DON BERNARDO.

> Please you to name it, sir.

DON CAMILLO.

> Sir, I have long held you in singular esteem: and what I
> shall now say, will be a proof of it. You know, sir, I have
> but one son.

DON BERNARDO.

Ay, sir.

DON CAMILLO.

And the fortune I am blessed withal, you pretty well know
what it is.

DON BERNARDO.

'Tis a fair one, sir.

DON CAMILLO.

Such as it is the whole reversion is my son's. He is now
engaged in his attendance on our master, the Duke. But e'er he
went he left me with the secret of his heart: his love for your
fair daughter. For your consent, he said, 'twas ready: I took a
while indeed to think upon it, and now have brought you
mine; and am come to bind the contract with half my fortune
in present, the whole some time hence, and in the meanwhile,
my hearty blessing. Ha? What say you to't, Don Bernard?

DON BERNARDO.

Why, really, neighbour, I must own, I have heard something
of this matter.

DON CAMILLO.

Heard something of it? No doubt, you have.

DON BERNARDO.

Yes, now I recollect it well.

DON CAMILLO.

Was it so long ago then?

DON BERNARDO.

Very long ago, neighbour – on Tuesday last.

DON CAMILLO.

What, am I mocked in this business, Don Bernardo?

DON BERNARDO.

Not mocked, good Camillo, not mocked: but in love matters,
you know, there are abundance of changes in half an hour.
Time, time, neighbour, plays tricks with all of us.

DON CAMILLO.

Time, sir! What tell you me of time? Come, I see how this
goes! Can a little time, take a man by the shoulder and shake
off his honour? Let me tell you, neighbour, it must either be
a strong wind or a very mellow honesty that drops so easily.
Time, quoth'a?

DON BERNARDO.

Look'ee Camillo; will you please to put your indignation in
your pocket for half a moment, while I tell you the whole
truth of the matter. My daughter, you must know, is such a
tender soul, she cannot possibly see a Duke's younger son
without falling desperately in love with him. Now you know,
neighbour, when greatness rides post after a man of my
years, 'tis both prudence and good breeding to let oneself be
overtaken by it. And who can help all this? I profess, it was
not my seeking, neighbour.

DON CAMILLO.

I profess, a fox might earth in the hollowness of your heart,
neighbour, and there's an end. If I were to give a bad
conscience its true likeness, it should be drawn after a very
near neighbour to a certain poor neighbour of yours. –
Neighbour! with a pox!

DON BERNARDO.

Nay, you are so nimble with me, you shall hear nothing.

DON CAMILLO.

Sir, if I will speak nothing, I will hear nothing. As for what
you have to say, if it come from your heart, it is a lie before
you speak it. – I'll to Luscinda; and if I find her in the same
story, why, I shall believe your wife was true to you, and
your daughter is your own. Fare you well.

DON BERNARDO.

Ay, but two words must go to that bargain. It happens, that I
am at present of opinion my daughter shall receive no more
company today, at least no such visits as yours.

Exeunt.

Scene Six

Enter LUSCINDA *above*.

LUSCINDA.
How tediously I have waited at the window,
Yet know not one that passes. – Should I trust
My letter to a stranger, whom I think
To bear an honest face (in which sometimes
We fancy we are wondrous skilful), then
I might be much deceived. This late example
Of base Fernando, bleeding in me now,
From each good aspect takes away my trust:
For his face seemed to promise truth and honour.
Since nature's gifts in noblest forms deceive,
Be happy you that wants 'em!

Enter CITIZEN.

                              Here comes one;
I've seen him, though I know him not; he has
An honest face too – that's no matter. – Sir –

CITIZEN.
To me?

LUSCINDA.
As you were of a virtuous maiden born
(There is no doubt you are), I do conjure you
Grant me one boon. Say, do you know me, sir?

CITIZEN.
Ay, Luscinda, and your worthy father.

LUSCINDA.
I have not time to press the suit I've to you
With many words; nay I should want the words,
Tho' I had leisure; but for love of justice,

And as you pity misery, – but I wander
Wide from my subject. You know Cardenio, sir?

CITIZEN.

Yes, very well, and love him too, as well.

LUSCINDA.

Oh, there an angel spake! Then I conjure you,
Convey this paper to him: and believe me,
You do Heaven service in it, and shall have cause
Not to repent your pains. – I know not what
Your fortune is; – pardon me, gentle sir,
That I am bold to offer this.

She offers a purse.

CITIZEN.

By no means, Lady –

DON BERNARDO (*within*).

Luscinda!

LUSCINDA.

I trust to you; Heaven put it in your heart
To work me some relief.

CITIZEN.

Doubt it not, lady. You have moved me so,
That though a thousand dangers barred my way,
I'd dare 'em all to serve you.

LUSCINDA.

Thanks from a richer hand than mine requite you!

Exit CITIZEN.

DON BERNARDO (*within*).

Why, daughter…

LUSCINDA.

I come: oh, Cardenio, feel but half my grief,
And thou wilt out fly time to bring relief.

Exit LUSCINDA *from the window.*

End of Act Two.

ACT THREE

Scene One

In the Palace.

Enter CITIZEN *and* CARDENIO.

CITIZEN.
    When from the window she did bow and call,
    Her passions shook her voice; and from her eyes,
    Beblubbered all with tears, a strange wildness
    Bespoke concern above a common sorrow.

CARDENIO.
    Poor Luscinda! Treacherous, damned Fernando!
    She bids me fill my memory with danger;
    I do, my Luscinda, yes I fill
    The region of my thought with nothing else;
    Lower, she tells me here, that this affair
    Shall yield a testimony of her love:
    And prays her letter may come safe and sudden.
    This prayer the heavens have heard, and I beseech 'em
    To hear all prayers she makes.

CITIZEN

                        Have patience, sir.

CARDENIO.
    O my good friend, methinks I am too patient.
    Is there a treachery like this in baseness
    Recorded anywhere? It is the deepest:
    None but itself can be its parallel:
    And from a friend professed! Friendship? Why 'tis
    A word forever maimed: he a friend?
    I'll make a horse my friend first. Thou goat!
    Whose lust is more insatiate than the grave.
    Such a villainy
    A writer could not put down in his scene,

Without taxation of his auditory
For fiction most enormous.

CITIZEN.

These upbraidings
Cool time while they are vented.

CARDENIO.

I am counselled.
For you, evermore thanks. You've done much for us;
So gently pressed to it that I may persuade me
You'll do a little more.

CITIZEN.

Put me t'employment
That's honest, tho' not safe, with my best spirits
I'll give t'accomplishment.

CARDENIO.

No more but this;
For I must see Luscinda and to appear
Like Cardenio, as I am, might haply spoil
Some good event ensuing. Let me crave
Th'exchange of habit with you: some disguise
May bear me to my love, unmarked, and secret.

CITIZEN.

You shall not want. Spur post and get you gone.
Take you my mule. Would he were Pegasus.

CARDENIO.

I thank you, sir, my rage shall give him wings.
O Luscinda! Stand but this rude shock;
Hold faith against the dread assault
Of this base lord, the service of my life
Shall be devoted to repay thy constancy.
O treacherous Fernando! Here,
Thou shalt pay me the injury thou didst.
These hands shall rend out the heart
In which do harbour and are heaped together,
All evils but principally fraud and deceit.

Exeunt.

Scene Two

DON BERNARDO*'s house. Preparations for a wedding are taking place.*

LUSCINDA *at the grilled window.*

LUSCINDA.
    I've hoped to the latest minute hope can give:
    He will not come: has not received my letter;
    May be some other view has from our home
    Repealed his changed eye: for what business can
    Excuse a tardiness thus wilful? None,
    Well then, it is not business. Oh that letter, –
    I say, is not delivered; or he's sick;
    Or – O suggestion, wherefore wilt thou fright me?
    On mere purpose, on plotted purpose;
    Cardenio to Fernando yields me up,
    And he hath chose another mistress.
    All presumptions make powerful to this point:
    His own protraction, Fernando left behind
    (That strain lacked jealousy, therefore lacked love);
    So sure as life shall empty itself in death,
    This new surmise is a bold certainty.
    Fernando would not, durst not thus infringe
    The law of friendship; thus provoke a man,
    That bears a sword, and wears his flag of youth
    As fresh as he; he durst not; 'tis contrivance,
    Gross-daubing 'twixt them both. But I'm overheard...

Enter CARDENIO, *muffled.*

CARDENIO.
    Stay Luscinda; has this outward veil
    Quite lost me to thy knowledge?

LUSCINDA.

O, Cardenio!
Thy presence ends the stern debate of doubt,
And cures me of a thousand heartsick fears,
Sprung from thy absence: yet awakes a train
Of other sleeping terrors. Do you weep?

CARDENIO.

Would I could weep;
For then mine eye would drop upon my heart
And 'suage the fire there.

LUSCINDA.

You are full possessed
How things go here. First welcome heartily;
Welcome to the ending of my last good hour:
Now summer's bliss and gaudy days are gone,
My lease in 'em's expired.

CARDENIO.

Not so, Luscinda.

LUSCINDA.

Yes, Cardenio, an everlasting storm
Is come upon me, which I can't bear out.
I cannot stay much talk; we have lost leisure;
And thus it is: your absence hath given breeding
To what my letter hath declared, and is
This instant on th'effecting.

Flourish within.

Hark, the music
Is now on tuning, which must celebrate
This business so discordant. Tell me then,
What will you do?

CARDENIO.

I know not what: advise me:
I'll kill the traitor.

LUSCINDA.
>   O! take heed: his death
> Betters our cause no whit. No killing, Cardenio.

CARDENIO.
> My blood stands still; and all my faculties
> Are by enchantment dulled. Your gracious powers
> The guardians of sworn faith, and suffering virtue,
> Inspire prevention of this dreaded mischief!
> This moment is our own; let's use it, love,
> And fly on the instant from this house of woe.

LUSCINDA.
> Alas! Impossible: my steps are watched;
> There's no escape for me. You must stay too.

CARDENIO.
> What! Stay, and see thee ravished from my arms?
> I'll force thy passage. Wear I not a sword?
> Ne'er on man's thigh rode better. If I suffer
> The traitor play his part; if I not do
> Manhood and justice, honour; let me be deemed
> A tame, pale coward, whom the night owl's hoot
> May turn to aspen leaf:

He unsheathes his sword.

>   Some man take this,
> Give me a distaff for it.

LUSCINDA.
>   Patience, Cardenio,
> And trust to me; I have fore-thought the means
> To disappoint these nuptials. Hark! again;
> These are the bells knoll for us. See the lights
> Move this way, Cardenio. Quick, behind yon arras,
> And take thy secret stand. Dispute it not;
> I have my reasons, you anon shall know them:
> There you may mark the passages of the night.
> Yet, more: I charge you bear the dearest ties

Whate'er you see, or hear, whate'er shall hap,
In your concealment rest a silent statue.
Nay, hide thee straight, or see, I'm armed and vow
To fall a bleeding sacrifice before thee.

Thrusts him out, to the arras.

I dare not tell thee of my purpose, Cardenio,
Lest it should wrap thee in such agonies,
Which my love could not look on.

Through one door servants enter with lights, followed by
FERNANDO, DON BERNARDO *and a* PRIEST.

FERNANDO.
How fares your daughter? My beauteous mistress?
What is she ready yet?

DON BERNARDO.
No doubt she'll lose no time, sir. Young maids in her way
Tread up thorns and think an hour an age
Till the priest has done his part.

LUSCINDA *enters.*

FERNANDO.
Why, Luscinda, wilt thou with this gloom
Darken my triumph; suffering discontent
And wan displeasure, to subdue that cheek
Where love should sit enthroned? Behold your slave;
Nay frown not; for each hour of growing time
Shall talk me to thy service, till by merit
Of dearest love I blot low-born Cardenio
From thy fair mind.

LUSCINDA.
                    So I shall make it foul;
This counsel is corrupt.

FERNANDO.
                    Come you will change.

LUSCINDA.

    Why would you make a wife of such a one,
    That is so apt to change? This foul proceeding
    Still speaks against itself, and vilifies
    The purest of your judgement. For your birth's sake
    I will not dart my hoarded curses at you,
    Nor give my meanings language: for the love
    Of all good things together, yet take heed,
    And spurn the tempter back.

DON BERNARDO.

    I think you're mad, perverse and foolish, wretch!

LUSCINDA.

    How may I be obedient and wise too?
    Of my obedience, sir, I cannot strip me;
    Nor can I then be wise: grace against grace!
    Ungracious, if I do not obey my father;
    Most perjured if I do. Yet, lord, consider,
    Or e'er too late, or e'er that knot be tied,
    Which may with violence damnable be broken,
    No other way dissever'd; yet consider,
    You wed my body, not my heart, my lord;
    No part of my affection. Sounds it well?
    'Cardenio's love is Lord Fernando's wife';
    Have you an ear for this harsh sound?

FERNANDO.

    No shot of reason can come near the place,
    Where my love's fortified. The day shall come,
    Wherein you'll chide this backwardness and bless
    Our fervour in this course.

LUSCINDA.

                 No, no, Fernando,
    When you shall find what prophet you are proved,
    You'll prophesy no more.

DON BERNARDO.

                Have done this talking,
    If you will cleave to your obedience, do't;

If not, unbolt the portal and begone;
My blessing stay behind you.

LUSCINDA.

                  Sir, your pardon
I will not swerve a hair's breath from my duty;
It shall first cost me dear.

DON BERNARDO.

                Well, then, to th'point:
Give me your hand. My honoured lord, receive
My daughter of me (nay no dragging back,
But with my curses); whom I frankly give you,
And wish you joy and honour.

PRIEST.

Don Fernando, will you take this woman, who is here
present, for your lawful spouse, according as our holy
mother, the Church, commands?

FERNANDO.

I will.

PRIEST.

Will you, Lady Luscinda, take this lord, Don Fernando, who
is here present, for your lawful spouse, according as our holy
mother, the Church, commands?

LUSCINDA *does not answer.*

CARDENIO (*aside*).

O Luscinda, consider what thou dost.
Thou canst not be another's, thou art mine.
O treacherous Fernando, thou shalt pay,
Death of my life...

PRIEST.

              My pretty mistress?

LUSCINDA.

                    Yea.

FERNANDO *puts on her ring; then coming to kiss her;*
LUSCINDA *faints.*

FERNANDO.

    She dies upon me! Help!

    General commotion. LUSCINDA *is carried out. Exeunt all*
    except CARDENIO.

CARDENIO.

    Lost, in an instant, in a little word.
    Abandoned by Heaven, devoid of counsel,
    Proclaimed an enemy unto the earth
    Which should uphold me: the air denies me
    Breath enough for my sighs, the water humour
    Sufficient to my eyes, only the fire
    Increases in such a manner that I
    Burn thoroughly with rage and jealousy.

    Ungenerous lord! You have wronged me much,
    Wrong'd me so basely, in so dear a point,
    As stains the cheek of honour with a blush;
    Cancels the bond of service; bids allegiance
    Throw to the wind all high respects of birth,
    Title and eminence; and in their stead
    Fills up my panting heart with just defiance.

    Why did I not thus challenge him and say
    'If you have sense of shame or justice, lord,
    Forgo this bad intent, or with your sword
    Answer me like a man, and I shall thank you:
    Cardenio once dead, Luscinda may
    Be thine, but living she's a prize too rich
    To part with'? Traitor, cozening Judas,
    The falsest friend that ever friendship knew!

    And cruel, ungrateful, scornful Luscinda,
    Mutable traitress, covetous of riches,
    Shuts up the eyes of her affection
    And renders it to him whom fortune loves.

    And I a coward who could not take revenge
    (Which with facility I could have done,
    As they suspected not my being there).
    I'll execute revenge upon myself,

And with more rigour give myself that pain
Which none but they deserve. Oh foolish sot,
To speak of what I should do, but did not.

I want no health without Luscinda, but
Since she forsakes me I must die. For as
She shows by her unfaithfulness that she
Desires my ruin, by suffering will I
Strive to convince her that a better fate
Did I deserve than false perjury.

Cardenio, struck though with injuries,
A wretch, to his own knowledge, almost lost,
Will leave this place, and like another Lot
Not daring to look back, will seek the dark
(And desolate there, the woods and rocks among),
Let slip my voice and there untie my tongue.

Exit.

Scene Three

Garden in DON BERNARDO'*s house. Immediately afterwards.*
Everyone surrounding LUSCINDA *in a swoon.*

DON BERNARDO.
  Throng not about her;
  But give her air.

FERNANDO (*aside*).
              My soul is all on fire;
  And burns impatient of this forced delay.

DON BERNARDO.
  Bow her head.

FERNANDO.
              What paper's that? Let's see it.

DUENNA.

   'Tis her own hand.

DON BERNARDO.

   'Tis but her fright, she will recover soon.
   My lord, this wild tumult soon will cease,
   The cause removed; and all return to calmness.
   Passions in women are as short in working,
   As strong in their effect. Let the priest wait.
   What learn you by that paper, good my lord?

FERNANDO.

   That she would do the violence to herself
   Which nature hath anticipated on her.
   She here declares she could not be my wife
   Because that she already is betrothed.
   What dagger means she? Search her well, I pray.

DUENNA.

   Here is the dagger.

DON BERNARDO.

              O, the stubborn sex.

   Rash e'en to madness!

FERNANDO.

            What, flout me?

DON BERNARDO.

   Life flows in her again.

FERNANDO.

           Perchance.

   FERNANDO *tries to stab* LUSCINDA.

DON BERNARDO.

           Hold! Seize him!

FERNANDO.

               Dogs!

   DON BERNARDO *and his servants restrain* FERNANDO,
   who breaks free and exits.

DON BERNARDO
      Take her to her chamber.
      But tend her as you would the world's best treasure.

      Exeunt.

Scene Four

Before DON CAMILLO'*s house. Morning.*

Enter PEDRO.

PEDRO.
      Cardenio's departure from the court,
      With the long doubtful absence of my brother
      (Who cannot suffer, but my father feels it);
      Have trusted me with strong suspicions,
      And dreams, that will not let me sleep, nor eat,
      Nor taste those recreations health demands:
      But like a whirlwind hither have they snatched me,
      Perforce to be resolved. I know my brother
      Had Cardenio's father for his host; from him
      Enquiry may befriend me.

      DON CAMILLO *enters.*

                              Old sir, I'm glad
      To've met you thus: what ails the man? Camillo?

DON CAMILLO.
      Ha?

PEDRO.
      Is't possible you should forget your friends?

DON CAMILLO.
      Friends? What are those?

PEDRO.
                              Why those that love you, sir.

DON CAMILLO.

You're none of those sure if you be Lord Pedro.

PEDRO.

Yes. I am that Lord Pedro, and I lie not,
If I protest, I love you passing well.

DON CAMILLO.

You loved my son too, passing well I take it;
One that believed too suddenly his court-creed.

PEDRO (*aside*).

All is not well. – Good old man, do not rail.

DON CAMILLO.

My lord, my lord, you've dealt dishonourably.

PEDRO.

Good sir, I am so far from doing wrongs
Of that base strain, I understand you not.

DON CAMILLO.

Indeed! You know not neither, o' my conscience,
How your most virtuous brother, noble Fernando
(You are so like him, lord, you are the worse;
Rots take such dissemblers!), under colour
Of buying horses, and I know not what,
Bought my poor boy out of possession
Ev'n of his plighted faith. Was not this honour?
And this a constant friend?

PEDRO.

                    I dare not say so.

DON CAMILLO.

Now you have robbed him of his love, take all;
Make up your malice and dispatch his life too.

PEDRO.

If you would hear me, sir…

DON CAMILLO.

                    Your brave old father
Would have been torn in pieces with wild horses,

Ere he had done this treachery. On my conscience,
Had he but dreamt you two would have committed
This base, unmanly crime…

PEDRO.

Why this is madness.

DON CAMILLO.
I've done, I've eased my heart, now you may talk.

PEDRO.
Then as I am a gentleman, believe me
(For I will lie for no man); I'm so far
From being guilty of the least suspicion
Of sin that way, that fearing the long absence
Of Cardenio and my brother might beget
Something to start at, hither have I travelled
To know the truth of you.

DOROTEA *enters behind*.

DOROTEA (*aside*).
Lord Pedro, and a stranger? These may give me
Some comfort from their talk. I'll step aside:
And hear what fame is stirring.

PEDRO.

Why this wondering?

DON CAMILLO.
Can there be one so near in blood as you
To that Fernando, and an honest man?

PEDRO.
While he was good I do confess my nearness;
But since his fall from honour, he's to me
As a strange face I saw but yesterday,
And as soon lost.

DON CAMILLO.
I ask your pardon, lord;
I was too rash and bold.

PEDRO.

No harm done, sir.

DON CAMILLO.

But is it possible you should not hear
The passage 'twixt Luscinda and your brother?

PEDRO.

None of all this.

Enter CITIZEN.

DON CAMILLO.

How now?

CITIZEN.

I bear you tidings, sir, which I could wish
Some other tongue delivered.

DON CAMILLO.

Whence, I pray you?

CITIZEN.

From your son, sir.

DON CAMILLO.

Cardenio? Where is he?

CITIZEN.

That's more than I know now, sir.
But this I can assure you, he has left
The city raging mad; Heaven comfort him!
He came to that cursed marriage, the fiends take it!

DON CAMILLO.

Prithee begone, and bid the bell knoll for me:
I have had one foot in the grave some time.
Nay go, good friend; thy news deserve no thanks.

Exit CITIZEN.

How does your lordship?

PEDRO.

                    That's well said, old man.
I hope all shall be well yet.

DON CAMILLO.

                    It had need;
For 'tis a crooked world. Farewell, poor boy!

Enter DON BERNARDO.

DON BERNARDO.

This comes of forcing women where they hate:
It was my own sin; and I am rewarded.
Now I am like an aged oak, alone,
Left for all tempest. I would cry, but cannot:
I'm dried to death almost with these vexations.
Oh, I could eat my heart and fling away
My soul for anguish.
Lord! What a heavy load I have within me!
My heart, my heart, my heart!

DON CAMILLO.

                    Has this ill weather
Met with thee too?

DON BERNARDO.

Till now I have not wept these thirty years.

DON CAMILLO.

Sure, every swine will have his Martinmas.

DON BERNARDO.

O wench, that I were with thee!

DON CAMILLO.

You do not come to mock at me now?

DON BERNARDO.

                    Ha?

DON CAMILLO.

Do not dissemble; thou mayst find a knave
As bad as thou art, to undo thee too:
I hope to see that day before I die yet.

DON BERNARDO.

    It needeth not, Camillo, I am knave
    Sufficient to myself. If thou wilt rail,
    Do it as bitterly as thou canst think of;
    For I deserve it. Take thy stick and strike me;
    And I will thank thee for't. I've lost my daughter;
    She's stolen away, and whither gone I know not.
    Grief is an impudent guest,
    A follower everywhere, a hanger-on,
    That words nor blows can drive away.

DON CAMILLO.

    She has a fair blessing in being from you, sir.
    I was too poor a brother for your greatness;
    You must be grafted into noble stocks,
    And have your titles raised. My state was laughed at:
    And my alliance scorned. I've lost a son too;
    Which must not be put up so.

Offers to draw.

PEDRO.

                   Hold, be counselled.
    You've equal losses; urge no farther anger.
    Heaven, pleased now at your love, may bring again
    And no doubt will, your children to your comforts:
    In which adventure my foot shall be foremost.
    And one more will I add, my honoured father;
    Who has a son to grieve for too, tho' tainted.
    Let your joint sorrow be as a balm to heal
    These wounds of adverse fortune.

DON BERNARDO.

                  Come, Camillo,
    Do not deny your love for charity;
    I ask it of you. Let this noble lord
    Make brothers of us, whom our own cross fates
    Could never join. What I have been, forget;
    What I intend to be, believe and nourish:
    I do confess my wrongs; give me your hand.

DON CAMILLO.

Heaven make thee honest; there.

PEDRO.

'Tis done like good men.
Now there rests nought, but that we part, and each
Take several ways in quest of our lost friends:
Some of my train o'er the wild rocks shall wait you.
Our best search ended, here we'll meet again
And tell the fortunes of our separate travels.

Exeunt.

DOROTEA.

I would your brother had but half your virtue!
Yet there remains a little spark of hope
That lights me to some comfort. The match is crossed;
The parties separate; and I again
May come to see this man that has betrayed me;
And wound his conscience for it. My father
Makes mighty offers yonder by a crier,
To anyone can bring me home again.
I will not go, whatever fortune guides me;
Tho' every step I went, I trod upon
Dangers as fearful and as pale as death.
No, no, Fernando; I will follow thee
Where there is day. Time may beget a wonder.

End of Act Three.

ACT FOUR

Scene One

In the Sierra Morena Mountains.

DOROTEA, *dressed as a shepherd, sings a love song. Three or four* SHEPHERDS *and the* MASTER *of the flock are all listening to her.*

Warily, CARDENIO *comes into view, and listens spellbound by* DOROTEA*'s song.* CARDENIO *is half-naked, has a dark, thick beard and long, messy hair…*

FIRST SHEPHERD.
 Heaven comfort him!

SECOND SHEPHERD.
 If he have a mother, I believe, neighbours, she's a
 woe-woman for him at this hour.

MASTER.
 Why should he haunt these wild unpeopled mountains,
 Where nothing dwells but hunger and sharp winds?

FIRST SHEPHERD.
 His melancholy, sir, that's the main devil of it. Go to, I fear
 he has had too much foul play offered him.

MASTER.
 How came he here?

FIRST SHEPHERD.
 In yonder stream, we found the carcass of a mule, half
 devoured by dogs and crows.

MASTER.
 How does he get his meat?

SECOND SHEPHERD.

Why now and then he takes our victuals from us, tho' we desire him to eat; and instead of a short grace, beats us well and soundly, then falls to.

MASTER.

Where lies he?

FIRST SHEPHERD.

E'en as night o'ertakes him.

MASTER.

Now will I be hanged, an some fair-snouted skittish woman, or other, be not at the end of this madness.

FIRST SHEPHERD.

Well if he be lodged within the sound of us, I knew our music would allure him.

SECOND SHEPHERD.

How attentively he stood, and how he fixed his eyes, when Florio – (*Referring to* DOROTEA.) sung his love ditty. Oh here he comes again.

Enter CARDENIO.

MASTER.

Let him alone; he wonders strangely at us. Look how his face is toasted by the sun!

FIRST SHEPHERD.

Not a word, sirs, to cross him, as you love your shoulders.

SECOND SHEPHERD.

He seems much disturbed: I believe the mad fit is upon him.

CARDENIO.

Horsemanship! Hell – riding should be abolished:
Turn the barb'd steeds loose to their native wildness;
It is a beast too noble to be made
The property of man's baseness. What a letter
Wrote he to his brother? What a man was I?
Why, Perseus did not know his seat like me;

The Parthian that rides swift without the rein,
Matched not my grace and firmness. Shall this lord
Die, when men pray for him? Think you 'tis meet?

FIRST SHEPHERD.

I do not know what to say. Neither I, nor all the confessors of
Spain can unriddle this wild stuff.

CARDENIO.

I must to court! Be ushered into grace,
By a large list of praises ready penn'd!
O Devil! What a venomous world is this,
When commendations are the baits to ruin!
All these good words, these gyves and fetters, sir,
To keep me bolted there: while the false sender
Played out the game of treachery. Hold; come hither;
You have an aspect, sir, of wond'rous wisdom,
And, as it seems, are travell'd deep in knowledge;
Have you e'er seen the phoenix of the earth
The bird of paradise?

SECOND SHEPHERD.

In troth, not I, sir.

CARDENIO.

I have; and known her haunts and where she built
Her spicy nest: till, like a credulous fool,
I showed the treasure to a friend in trust,
And he hath robbed me of her. Trust no friend:
Keep thy heart's counsels close. Hast thou a mistress?
Give her not out in words; nor let thy pride
Be wanton to display her charms to view;
Love is contagious: and a breath of praise,
Or a slight glance, has kindled up its flame,
And turned a friend a traitor. 'Tis in proof;
And it has hurt my brain.

FIRST SHEPHERD.

Marry, now there is some moral in his madness, and we may
profit by it.

SECOND SHEPHERD.

    I think his skull's as empty as a sucked egg.

MASTER.

    See he grows cool and pensive.

    Go towards him, boy, but do not look that way.

DOROTEA.

    Alas! I tremble.

CARDENIO.

    Oh, my pretty youth!

    Come hither, child; did not your song imply

    Something of love?

FIRST SHEPHERD.

    Ha-ha – goes it there? Now if the boy be witty, we shall trace
    something.

DOROTEA.

    Yes, sir, it was the subject.

CARDENIO.

    Sit here then; come, shake not, good pretty soul,

    Nor do not fear me; I'll not do thee wrong.

DOROTEA.

    Why do you look so on me?

CARDENIO.

                   I have reasons.

    It puzzles my philosophy to think

    That the rude blast, hot sun, and lashing rains

    Have made no fiercer war upon thy youth;

    Nor hurt the bloom of that vermillion cheek.

    You weep too, do you not?

DOROTEA.

                 Sometimes, I do.

CARDENIO.

    I weep sometimes too. You're extremely young.

DOROTEA.

Indeed I've seen more sorrows far than years.

CARDENIO.

Yet all these have not broken your complexion.
You have a strong heart, and you are happier.
I warrant, you're a very loving woman.

DOROTEA.

A woman, sir? (*Aside.*) I fear has found me out.

SECOND SHEPHERD.

He takes the boy for a woman. Mad again!

CARDENIO.

You've met some disappointment; some foul play
Has crossed your love. I read it in your face.

DOROTEA.

You read a truth then.

CARDENIO.

              Where can lie the fault?
Is't in the man, or some dissembling knave,
He put in trust? Ho! Have I hit the cause?

DOROTEA.

You're not far off.

CARDENIO.

This world is full of coz'ners, very full;
Young virgins must be wary in their ways.
I've known a duke's son do as great a knavery.
Will you be ruled by me?

DOROTEA.

              Yes.

CARDENIO.

              Kill yourself.
'Twill be a terror to the villain's conscience
The longest day he lives.

DOROTEA.

By no means, what?
Commit self-murder!

CARDENIO.

Yes, I'll have it so.

FIRST SHEPHERD.

I fear his fit is returning. Take heed of all hands. Sir, do you want anything?

CARDENIO.

Thou lie'st; thou canst not hurt me: I am proof
'Gainst farther wrongs. Steal close behind me, lady,
I will avenge thee.

DOROTEA.

Thank the heavens, I'm free.

CARDENIO.

O treacherous, base Fernando! Have I caught thee?

CARDENIO *seizes on the* SECOND SHEPHERD.

SECOND SHEPHERD.

Help! Help! Good neighbours; he will kill me else.

DOROTEA *runs out.*

CARDENIO.

Here, thou shalt pay thy heart blood for the wrongs
Thou heap'd upon this head. Faith-breaker! Villain!
I'll suck thy life blood.

FIRST SHEPHERD.

Good sir, have patience, this is no Fernando.

They rescue the SECOND SHEPHERD.

CARDENIO.

Well, let him slink to court and hide a coward;
Not all his father's guards shall shield him there.
Or if he prove too strong for mortal arm,
I will solicit every saint in Heav'n
To lend me vengeance. I'll about it straight.

The wrathful elements shall wage this war;
Furies shall haunt him; vultures gnaw his heart;
And nature pour forth all her store of plagues,
To join in punishment of trust betrayed.

Exit CARDENIO.

SECOND SHEPHERD.
Go thy ways, and a vengeance go with thee!
Pray, feel my nose, is it fast, neighbours?

FIRST SHEPHERD.
'Tis as well as may be.

SECOND SHEPHERD.
He pulled at it as he would have dragged a bullock backward
by the tail. An't had been some men's noses that I know,
neighbours, who knows where it had been now? He has
given me such a devilish dash o'er the mouth that I feel I
shall never whistle to my sheep again: then they'll make
holy-day.

FIRST SHEPHERD.
Come, shall we go?

SECOND SHEPHERD.
Aye, for I fear, if the youth come again, our second course
will be much more against our stomachs.

FIRST SHEPHERD.
Tush, tush! Come, go we.

SECOND SHEPHERD.
Whither?

FIRST SHEPHERD.
Come, let's search until we find him, and being found, either
by force or fair means we will carry him to Almodovar
which is but eight leagues hence, and there we will have him
cured if his disease may be helped, or at least we shall learn
what he is when he turns to his wits, and whether he have
any friends to whom notice of his misfortune may be given.

MASTER.

Walk you afore; I will but give my boy
Some short instructions, and I'll follow straight.
We'll crash a cup together.

FIRST SHEPHERD.

Pray, do not linger.

MASTER.

I will not, sirs.

SHEPHERDS *exeunt*.

This must not be a boy;
His voice, mien, gesture, everything he does,
Savours of soft and female delicacy,
He but puts on this seeming, and his garb
Speaks him of such a rank, as well persuades me,
He plays the swain rather to cloak some purpose,
Than forced to't by a need: I've waited long
To mark the end he has in this disguise;
But am not perfect in't. The madman's coil
Has driven him shaking hence. These fears betray him.
If he prove right, I'm happy. O, he's here.

Enter DOROTEA.

Come hither, boy; where did you leave the flock, child?

DOROTEA.

Grazing below, sir. (*Aside*.) What does he mean to stroke
one's cheek so? I hope I'm not betrayed.

MASTER.

Have you learnt the whistle yet, and when to fold?
And how to make the dog bring in the strayers?

DOROTEA.

Time, sir, will furnish me with all these rules;
My will is able, but my knowledge weak, sir.

MASTER.

That's a good child: why dost thou blush, my boy?
(*Aside*.) 'Tis certainly a woman. Speak, my boy.

DOROTEA.

Heav'n, how I tremble. 'Tis unusual to me
To find such kindness at a master's hand,
That am a poor boy, every way unable,
Unless it be in prayers, to merit it.
Besides, I've often heard old people say,
Too much indulgence makes boys rude and saucy.

MASTER.

Are you so cunning!

DOROTEA (*aside*).

How his eyes shake fire,
And measure every piece of youth about me!
The ewes want water, sir: shall I go drive 'em
Down to the cisterns? Shall I make haste, sir?
(*Aside*.) Would I were five miles from him – how he gripes
me!

MASTER.

Come, come, all this is not sufficient, child,
To make a fool of me. This is a fine hand,
A fine delicate hand – never change colour;
You understand me, and a woman's hand.

DOROTEA.

You're strangely out: yet if I were a woman,
I know, you are so honest and so good,
That tho' I wore disguise for some ends
You would not wrong me...

MASTER.

Come, you're made for love;
Will you comply? I'm madder with this talk.
There's nothing you can say, can take my edge off.

DOROTEA.

Oh, do but quench these foul affections in you,
That, like base thieves, have robb'd you of reason,
And I will be a woman; and begin
So sad a story, that if there be aught

Of human in you, or a soul that's gentle,
You cannot choose but pity my lost youth.

MASTER.

No stories now.

DOROTEA.

          Kill me directly, sir;
And you have any goodness, take my life.

PEDRO (*within*).

Hoa! Shepherd, will you hear me, sir?

MASTER.

What brawling rogue is that, in the Devil's name?

DOROTEA.

Blessing upon him, whatso'er he be!

    DOROTEA *runs out as* PEDRO *enters*.

PEDRO.

Good even, my friend; I thought you all had been asleep in
this country.

MASTER.

You had lied then, for you were waking when you thought so.

PEDRO.

I thank you, sir.

MASTER.

I pray you be covered; 'tis not so much worth, sir.

PEDRO.

Was that thy boy that ran away crying?

MASTER.

Yes; what then?

PEDRO.

Why dost thou beat him so?

MASTER.

To make him grow.

PEDRO.

A pretty medicine! Thou canst not tell me the way to the next nunnery?

MASTER.

How do you know that? Yes I can tell you: but the question is, whether I will or no; and indeed, I will not. Fare you well.

Exit MASTER.

PEDRO.

What a brute fellow's this? Are they all thus?
My brother Fernando tells me by his letters,
The mistress of his soul, the fair Luscinde,
Not far from hence hath taken sanctuary:
From which he prays my aid to bring her back.
I wear some doubts. But here it is appointed
We should meet; it must be here; 'tis so.
He comes.

Enter FERNANDO.

Now brother, what's this post-haste business
You hurry me about? Some wenching matter...

FERNANDO.

My letter told you, sir.

PEDRO.

'Tis true, it tells me, that you've lost a mistress
Whom your heart bleeds for; but the means to win her
From her close life, I take it, is not mentioned.
You're ever in these troubles.

FERNANDO.

                    Noble brother,

I own, I have too freely given scope
To youth's intemperate heat, and rash desires:
But think not, that I would engage your virtues
To any cause, wherein my constant heart
Attended not my eye. Till now my passions
Reign'd in my blood; ne'er pierced into my mind;

But I'm a convert grown to purest thoughts:
And must in anguish spend my days to come,
If I possess not her: so much I love.

PEDRO.

The means? She's in a cloister, is she not?
Within whose walls to enter as we are,
Will never be: few men, but friars come there;
Which we shall never make.

FERNANDO.

But for my Luscinda

I would *make* anything.

PEDRO.

Are you so hot?

FERNANDO.

Ho, Gerardo!

Enter GERARDO *and another dressed as a friar. He is carrying two more habits.* FERNANDO *hands the habit to his brother.*

Here, 'brother', as thou art and shalt then be.

Both start to dress in the habits.

PEDRO.

Be plainer with me, brother, what's your plan?

FERNANDO.

We must pretend, we do transport a body
As 'twere to's funeral: and coming late by,
Crave a night's leave to rest the hearse i'th'convent.
That be our course; for to such charity
Strict zeal and custom of the house give way.

PEDRO.

To feign a corpse – by the mass, 'twill never be.

FERNANDO.

And, opportune, a vacant hearse passed by
From rites but new performed, this very morn.

This for a price we hired, to put our scheme in act.
When we're once lodged, the means of her conveyance,
By safe and secret force, with ease we'll compass.

PEDRO (*aside*).
　　I'll serve him, be it but to save his honour.
　　But, brother, know my terms. If that your mistress
　　Will to the world come back, and she appear
　　An object worthy in our father's eye,
　　Woo her and win her; but if his consent
　　Keep not pace with your purpose...

FERNANDO.
　　　　　　　　　　　　Doubt it not.
　　I've looked not with a common eye, but chose
　　A noble virgin, who to make her so
　　Has all the gifts of Heaven and Earth upon her.
　　If ever woman yet could be an angel,
　　She is the nearest.

PEDRO.
　　　　　　　Well, a lover's praise
　　Feasts not a common ear.

FERNANDO.
　　　　　　　　　Now to our plot;
　　We shall bring night in with us.

　　Exeunt.

Scene Two

Enter CARDENIO *and the two* SHEPHERDS.

FIRST SHEPHERD.
  Good sir, compose yourself.

CARDENIO.
                    O Luscinda,
  That Heaven had made thee stronger than a woman,
  How happy had I been!

FIRST SHEPHERD.
                    He's calm again:
  I'll take this interval to work upon him.
  These wild and solitary places, sir
  But feed your pain; let better reason guide you;
  And quit this forlorn state, that yields no comfort.

  Lute sounds within.

CARDENIO.
  Ha! Hark, a sound from Heav'n! Do you hear nothing?

FIRST SHEPHERD.
  Yes, sir; the touch of some sweet instrument.

SECOND SHEPHERD.
  Here's no inhabitant.

CARDENIO.
                    No, no the better.

FIRST SHEPHERD.
  This is a strange place to hear music in.

CARDENIO.
  I'm often visited with these sweet airs.
  The spirit of some hapless man that died,

And left his love hid in a faithless woman,
Sure haunts these mountains.

DOROTEA *sings within*.

DOROTEA (*singing*).
Fond echo! Forego thy light strain,
And heedfully hear a lost maid;
Go, tell the false ear of the swain
How deeply his vows have betrayed.
Go tell him, what sorrows I bear,
See yet if his heart feel my woe:
'Tis now he must heal my despair,
Or death will make pity to flow.

FIRST SHEPHERD.
See, how his soul strives within him!

SECOND SHEPHERD.
                                    This sad strain
Has searched him to the heart.

CARDENIO.
                                    Excellent sorrow!
You never loved?

BOTH SHEPHERDS.
                    No.

CARDENIO.
                    Peace; and learn to grieve then.

DOROTEA *sings again*.

DOROTEA (*singing*).
Go, tell him what sorrows I bear:
See, yet if his heart feel my woe:
'Tis now he must heal my despair,
Or death will make pity to flow.

CARDENIO.
Is not this heavenly?

FIRST SHEPHERD.
                    I never heard the like, sir.

SECOND SHEPHERD (*aside*).
  But sure, is that not Florio?

CARDENIO.
  I'll tell you, my good friends; but pray say nothing;
  I'm strangely touched by this. The heavenly sound
  Diffuses a sweet peace through all my soul.
  But yet I wonder what new sad companion
  Grief has brought hither to outbid my sorrows.
  Stand off, stand off, stand off... Friends, it appears.

  Enter DOROTEA.

DOROTEA.
  How much more grateful are these craggy mountains,
  And these wild trees, than things of nobler natures,
  For these receive my plaints, and mourn again
  In many echoes to me. All good people
  Are fallen asleep; for ever. None are left,
  That have the sense and touch of tenderness
  For virtue's sake, no, scarce the memory,
  From whom I may expect counsel in fears,
  Ease to complainings, or redress of wrongs.

CARDENIO.
  This is a moving sorrow, but say nothing.

DOROTEA.
  What dangers have I run, and to what insults
  Exposed this ruin of my self? Oh! Mischief
  On that spotted hind, my vicious master!
  Who would have thought, that such poor worms as they
  (Whose best feed is coarse bread; whose beverage water);
  Should have so much rank blood? I shake all over,
  And blush to think what had become of me,
  If that good man had not relieved me from him.

CARDENIO.
  Since she is not Luscinda, she is heavenly.
  When she speaks next, listen as seriously
  As women do that have their loves at sea
  What wind blows every morning.

DOROTEA.

I cannot get this false man's memory
Out of my mind. You maidens, that shall live
To hear my mournful tale, when I am ashes,
Be wise; and to an oath no more give credit,
To tears, to vows (false both!) or any thing
A man shall promise, than to clouds, that now
Bear such a pleasing shape, and now are nothing.
For they will cozen (if they may be cozen'd)
The very gods they worship. Valour, justice,
Discretion, honesty, and all they covet,
To make them seeming saints, are but the wiles
By which these sirens lure us to destruction.

CARDENIO.

Do not you weep now? I could drop myself
Into a fountain for her.

FIRST SHEPHERD.

She weeps extremely.

CARDENIO.

Let her weep; 'tis well:
Her heart will break else. Great sorrows live in tears.

DOROTEA.

O false Fernando!

CARDENIO.

Ha!

DOROTEA.

And, oh, thou fool,
Forsaken Dorotea! Whose belief
And childish love have made thee so – go die;
For there is nothing left thee now to look for,
That can bring comfort, but a quiet grave.
There are all the miseries I long have felt,
And those to come, shall sweetly sleep together.
Fortune may guide that false Fernando hither,
To weep repentance o'er my pale dead corse,
And cheer my wandering spirit with those lov'd obsequies.

CARDENIO.

    Stay, lady, stay: can it be possible
    That you are Dorotea?

DOROTEA.

                That lost name,
    Spoken by one that needs must know my fortunes,
    Has taken much fear from me. Who are you, sir?
    For sure I am that hopeless Dorotea.

CARDENIO.

    And I, as far from any earthly comfort
    That I know yet, much wronged Cardenio!

DOROTEA.

    Cardenio!

CARDENIO.

    I once was thought so. If the cursed Fernando
    Had power to change you to a boy, why, lady,
    Should not that mischief make me anything
    That have an equal share in all the miseries
    His crimes have flung upon us?

DOROTEA.

                Well I know it:
    And pardon me, I could not know your virtues
    Before your griefs. Methought, when last we met,
    The accent of your voice struck on my ear
    Like something I had known, but floods of sorrows
    Drown'd the remembrance. If you'll please to sit
    (Since I have found a suffering true companion),
    And give me hearing, I will tell you something
    Of Luscinda that may comfort you.

CARDENIO.

    Blessing upon thee, if Heaven say Amen.
    But, soft! Let's shift our ground, guide but our sad steps
    To some remoter gloom, where, undisturb'd
    We may compare our woes; dwell on the tale
    Of mutual injuries, till our eyes run o'er,
    And we infect each other with fresh sorrows

Talked you of comfort? 'Tis the food of fools,
And we'll have none on't; but indulge despair:
So worn with griefs, steal to the cave of death,
And in a sigh give up our latest breath.

Scene Three

Evening. In the cloister of a convent.

LUSCINDA *is dressed in a nun's habit.*

LUSCINDA.
This quiet convent, hidden in the fields
Must be the place where I bewail my loss,
And here I'll waste all my remaining days
If with Cardenio I cannot be.
This wretched letter's all I've left of him;
I read it o'er and o'er through stinging tears.
'Ingrate' he calls me, 'enemy adored'.
O would that I could make him understand.
(*Reading the torn letter.*)
'Luscinda, thy false promise carries me
To such a place from whence thou sooner shalt
Hear news of my death than my just complaints.
Thou hast disdained me for one that hath more
But not for one that is worth more than I;
By thy beauty I deemed thee an angel,
By thy works I know thou art a woman.
Rest in peace (O causer of my war!).'

To whom now shall I cry? What power thus kneel to?
Deaf, deaf you saints of goodness, deaf to me?
Deaf, Heaven, to all my cries? Deaf, hope? Deaf, justice?
I am abused, and you that see all, saw it.
Saw it and smiled upon the villain that did it,
Saw it and gave him strength; why have I prayed to ye?

O Cardenio! The world shall come to know,
That loyal to my husband I did stay
To the last moment it was possible.

Treach'rous lord, when did Luscinda e'er
Give or a word or sign to make you think
That you had e'en the slightest hope at all
Of satisfying your base desire? When?

When did I not reject your amorous words
And harshly reprimand your bad intent?

But lust cannot burn bright without some hope
And doubtless I am partly then to blame,
Am guilty of some foolish carelessness
That prompted this impertinence in him,
If so, I must do penance for his crime.

The chapel bells ring.

May God preserve us all!

Enter another NOVICE.

                              What mean these bells
That toll this dirge, as for a funeral?

NOVICE.
Some friars bring a soul to burial.
They were to spend the night without these walls
But they have begged our gracious leave to stay
And harbour here until the morning breaks.

LUSCINDA.
How died he? Was he killed? Who murdered him?

NOVICE.
God, through his horse, that flung him to the floor.

LUSCINDA
Pray, sister, say the dead man's name again?

NOVICE.
I did not say't, nor have they told it me
Or, if they have, I was not listening.

But seems he was a noble gentleman.
What ails thee now? See, they are entering.

Enter PEDRO, GERARDO *and two others dressed as friars,*
carrying the coffin.

LUSCINDA.
Who is the dead man, brothers? Who is he?

They leave the coffin and exit.

NOVICE.
Rest, 'Tis bad to exercise the brain so much.

Exit the NOVICE.

LUSCINDA.
Cardenio... It surely cannot be.
O blessed Mary, true Mother of God,
I beg Cardenio, where'er he be
Is not where my fond soul says he lies.
But rather let him rest in Heaven high.
There is no memory that time cannot
Erase or pain that will not be consumed
By death. Why do I yield to these wild thoughts?

Your fear deceives your very eyes and ears,
For terror and despair can blind the sense,
And make them to suppose that which is not.
Let not your heart imagine what you fear
But move a little further off and leave
The dead man to himself alone, for he
Will have so much to speak about with God.

Suddenly the coffin opens and FERNANDO *jumps out.*

FERNANDO.
Come, 'sister', this is all as it may be
Devoutly witness, pray, my holy vow.
I too beg converse with divinity:
Divine Luscinda. Have I found thee now.

FERNANDO *stifles* LUSCINDA*'s scream, pushes her into*
the coffin and with his accomplices, carries her away.

End of Act Four.

ACT FIVE

Scene One

Later.

Enter PEDRO, LUSCINDA *and* FERNANDO.

PEDRO.
    Rest, certain, lady, nothing shall betide you
    But fair and noble usage. Pardon me,
    That hitherto a course of violence
    Has snatched you from that seat of contemplation
    To which you gave your afterlife.

LUSCINDA.

                    Where am I?

PEDRO.
    Not in the nunnery, never blush, nor tremble;
    Your honour has as fair a guard as when
    Within a cloister. Know then, what is done
    (Which, I presume, you understand not truly),
    Has this use, to preserve the life of one
    Dying for love of you, my brother and your friend:
    Under which colour we desired to rest
    Our hearse one night within the hallowed walls,
    Where you were surprised.

LUSCINDA.

               Are you that Lord Pedro
    So spoken of for virtue and fair life,
    And dare you lose these to be advocate
    For such a brother, such a sinful brother,
    Such an unfaithful treacherous brutal brother?

PEDRO.
    This is a fearful charge. (*Looks at* FERNANDO.)

LUSCINDA.

                    If you would have me
Think you still bear respect for virtue's name;
As you would wish your daughters, thus distressed
Might find a guard, protect me from Fernando
And I am happy.

PEDRO.

                    Come, sir, make your answer;
For as I have a soul, I am ashamed on't.

FERNANDO.

O Luscinda! See, thus self-condemned,
I throw me at your feet and sue for mercy.
If I have err'd, impute it to my love:
That tyrant god that bows us to his sway,
Rebellious to the laws of reasoning men,
That will not have his vot'ries action scanned,
But calls it justice when we most obey him.
He but commanded, when your eyes inspir'd;
Whose sacred beams, darted into my soul,
Have purged the mansion from impure desires,
And kindled in my heart a vestal's flame.

LUSCINDA.

Rise, rise, my lord; this well-dissembled passion
Has gained you nothing but a deeper hate.
Should I imagine he can truly love me,
That, like a villain, murthers my desires?
Where is Cardenio? What has thou done?

PEDRO.

Draw this way, lady;
I am not perfect in your story yet;
But see you've had some wrongs that want redress.
Only you must have patience to go with us
To yon small lodge which meets the sight from hence,
Where your distress shall find but due respect:
Till when, your griefs shall govern me as much
As nearness and affection to my brother.
Call my attendants yours, and use them freely;

For as I am a gentleman, no pow'r
Above your own will shall come near your person.
Look to the lady there. I follow straight.

As they are going out, DOROTEA *enters and plucks*
PEDRO *by the sleeve; the rest go out.*

DOROTEA.
Your ear a moment. Scorn not my tender youth.

PEDRO.
Look to the lady there. I follow straight.
What ails this boy? Why dost thou single me?

DOROTEA.
The due observance of your noble virtue,
Vowed to this mourning virgin, makes me bold
To give it more employment.

PEDRO.
                    Art thou not
The surly shepherd's boy, ran crying by me?

DOROTEA.
Yes, sir. And I thank Heaven and you for helping me.

PEDRO.
How did I help thee, boy?

DOROTEA.
I do not seem so, sir; and am indeed
A woman; one your brother once has loved,
Or, heaven forgive him else, he lied extremely.

PEDRO.
Weep not, good maid, O this licentious brother!
But how came you, a wanderer on these mountains?

DOROTEA.
That, as we pass, an't please you, I'll discover.
I will assure you, sir, these barren mountains
Hold many wonders of your brother's making.
Here wanders hapless Cardenio, worthy man!
Besides himself with wrongs...

PEDRO.

That name again...?

DOROTEA.
Sir, I said, Cardenio. Sleep weigh'd down his eyelids
Oppressed with watching, just as you approached us.

PEDRO.
O my brother! We shall sound the depths of falsehood.
If this be true! No more, but guide me to him:
I hope a fair end will succeed all yet.
I'll see him served first. Maid, you have overjoy'd me.
Thou shalt have right too: make thy fair appeal
To the good Duke, and doubt not but thy tears
Shall be repaid with interest from his justice.
Lead me to Cardenio.

Exeunt.

Scene Two

Enter the DUKE, DON BERNARDO *and* DON CAMILLO.

DON CAMILLO.
Ay, then your grace had had a son more; he a daughter; and I,
an heir: but let it be as 'tis, I cannot mend it; one way or
other I shall rub it over with rubbing to my grave, and there's
an end on't.

DUKE.
Our sorrows cannot help us, gentlemen.

DON CAMILLO.
Hang me, sir, if I shed one tear more. By Jove, I've wept so
long, I'm as blind as justice. When I come to see my hawks
(which I held a toy next to my son) if they be but house-high,
I must stand aiming at them like a gunner.

DUKE.
Why, he mourns like a man. Don Bernardo, you
Are still like April, full of showers and dews,
And yet I blame you not; for I myself
Feel the selfsame affections. Let them go;
They're disobedient children.

DON BERNARDO.
                              Ay, my lord;
Yet they may turn again.

DON CAMILLO.
Let them even have their swing; they're young and wanton;
the next storm we shall have them gallop homeward,
whining as pigs do in the wind.

DON BERNARDO.
Would I had my daughter any way.

DON CAMILLO.
Would'st thou have her with bairn, man, tell me that?

DON BERNARDO.
I care not, if an honest father got it.

DON CAMILLO.
You might have had her so in this good time,
Had my son had her: now you may go seek
Your fool to stop a gap with.

DUKE.
You say that Pedro charged you here should wait him:
He has o'erslipped the time, at which his letters
Of speed request that I should also meet him.
I fear some bad event is ushered in
By this delay.

Enter GERARDO.

GERARDO.
So please your grace,
Lord Pedro makes his approach.

DUKE.
> I thank thee fellow,
> For thy so timely news: comes he alone?

GERARDO.
> No, sir, attended well; and in his train
> Follows a hearse with all due rites of mourning.

Exit GERARDO.

DON BERNARDO.
> A hearse!

DUKE.
> Heaven fend Fernando live!

DON CAMILLO.
>   'Tis my Cardenio.

Enter PEDRO *hastily.*

DUKE.
> O welcome, welcome,
> Welcome, good Pedro! Say, what news?

DON CAMILLO.
> Do you bring joy or grief, my lord? For me,
> Come what can come, I'll live a month or two
> If the gout please, curse my physician once more,
> And then...

> *'Under this stone*
> *Lies seventy-one.'*

PEDRO.
> Signior, you do express a manly patience.
> My noble father, something I have brought
> To ease your sorrows: my endeavours have not
> Been altogether barren in my journey.

DUKE.
> It comes at need, boy; but I hoped it from thee.

Enter LUSCINDA, *veiled,* FERNANDO *behind, and attendants.*

PEDRO.

The company I bring will bear me witness
The busiest of my time has been employed
On this good task. Don Bernardo finds beneath
This veil his daughter; you my royal father,
Behind that lady find a wandering son.
How I met with them, and how brought them hither,
More leisure must enfold.

FERNANDO.

My father here!
And Cardenio's! O confusion! low as earth
(*To the* DUKE.) I bow me to your pardon.

DON BERNARDO.

O my girl!
Thou bring'st new life.

DUKE.

And you, my son, restore me
One comfort here that has been missing long.
I hope thy follies thou hast left abroad.

DON CAMILLO.

Ay, ay; you've all comforts but I; you have ruined me,
killed my poor boy; cheated and ruined him; and I have no
comfort.

PEDRO.

Be patient, signior; time may guide my hand
To work your comfort too.

DON CAMILLO.

I thank your lordship;
Would Grandsire Time have been so kind to've done it,
We might have joyed together like good fellows;
But he's so full of business, good old man,
'Tis wonder he could do the good he's done.

DON BERNARDO.

Nay, child, be comforted. These tears distract me.

DUKE.

Hear your good father, lady.

LUSCINDA.

Willingly.

DUKE.

The voice of parents is the voice of gods:
For to their children they are Heaven's lieutenants:
Made fathers, not for common uses merely
Of procreation (beasts and birds would be
As noble then as we); but to steer
The wanton freight of youth thro' storms and dangers,
Which with full sails they bear upon, and straighten
The moral line of life they bend so often:
For these are we made fathers, and for these
May challenge duty on our children's part.
Obedience is the sacrifice of angels,
Whose form you carry.

DON BERNARDO.

Hear the Duke, good wench.

LUSCINDA.

I do most heedfully. (*To the* DUKE.) My gracious lord,
Let me be so unmannered to request
He would not farther press me with persuasions
O' th'instant hour; but have the gentle patience
To bury this keen suit, till I shake hands
With my old sorrows...

DON CAMILLO.

Why dost look at me?

Alas! I cannot help thee.

LUSCINDA.

And but weep
A farewell to my murdered Cardenio.

DON CAMILLO.
  Blessing be with thy soul whene'er it leaves thee!

LUSCINDA.
  For such sad rites must be performed, my lord
  E'er I can love again. Maids that have loved,
  If they be worth that noble testimony,
  Wear their loves here, my lord, here in their hearts;
  Deep, deep within; not in their eyes, or accents;
  Such may be slipped away; or with true tears
  Washed out of all remembrance: mine, no physic
  But time or death can cure.

FERNANDO.
  You make your own conditions, and I seal them
  Thus on your virtuous hand.

DON CAMILLO.
                        Well, wench, thy equal
  Shall not be found in haste; I give thee that:
  Thou art a right one, ev'ry inch. Thy father
  (For without doubt, that snuff ne'er begot thee)
  Was some choice fellow, some true gentleman;
  I give thy mother thanks for't, – there's no harm done.
  Would I were young again, and had but thee,
  A good horse under me, and a good sword,
  And thus much for inheritance.

  DOROTEA *offers to show herself, but goes back.*

DUKE.
                        What boy's that
  Has offer'd twice or thrice to break upon us?
  I've noted him, and still he falls back fearful.

PEDRO.
  A little boy, sir, like a shepherd?

DUKE.
                        Yes.

PEDRO.
  'Tis your page, brother; one that was so, late.

FERNANDO.
  My page! What page?

PEDRO.
  Even so he says, your page;
  And more and worse, you stole him from his friends,
  And promised him preferment.

FERNANDO.
                    I, preferment?

PEDRO.
  And on some slight occasion let him slip
  Here on these mountains, where he had been starved
  Had not my people found him as we travelled.
  This was not handsome, brother.

FERNANDO.
                    You are merry.

PEDRO.
  You'll find it sober truth.

DUKE.
                    If so, 'tis ill.

FERNANDO.
  'Tis fiction all, sir – brother, you must please
  To look some other fool to put these tricks on;
  They are too obvious: please your grace, give leave
  T'admit the boy; if he know me and say
  I stole him from his friends, and cast him off,
  Know me no more. Brother, pray do not wrong me.

  DOROTEA *enters*.

PEDRO.
  Here is the boy. If he deny this to you
  Then I have wronged you.

DUKE.
  Hear me: what's thy name, boy?

DOROTEA.
  Florio, an't like your grace.

DUKE.

A pretty child.
Where wast thou born?

DOROTEA.

On t'other side of the mountains.

DUKE.

What are thy friends?

DOROTEA.

A father, sir; but poor.

DUKE.

How camest thou hither? How to leave thy father?

DOROTEA.

That noble gentleman pleased once to like me.
And, not to lie, so much to dote upon me,
That with his promises he won my youth
And duty from my father: him I followed.

PEDRO.

How say you now, brother?

DON CAMILLO.

Ay, my lord, how say you?

FERNANDO.

As I have life and soul, 'tis all a trick, sir.
I never saw the boy before.

DOROTEA.

O, sir,
Call not your soul to witness in a wrong:
And 'tis not noble in you to despise
What you have made thus. If I lie, let justice
Turn all her rods upon me.

DUKE.

Fie, Fernando;
There is no trace of cunning in this boy.

DON CAMILLO.

A good boy! Be not fearful: speak thy mind, child.
Nature, sure, meant thou should'st have been a wench;
And then't had been no marvel he had bobb'd thee!

DUKE.

Why did he put thee from him?

DOROTEA.

That to me
Is yet unknown, sir; for my faith he could not,
I never did deceive him; for my service
He had no just cause; what my youth was able
My will still put in act to please my master.
I cannot steal, therefore that can be nothing
To my undoing: no, nor lie; my breeding
Tho' it be plain, is honest.

DUKE.

Weep not, child.

DON CAMILLO.

This lord has abused men, women and children already: what
farther plot he has, the Devil knows.

DUKE.

If thou canst bring a witness of thy wrong
(Else it would be injustice to believe thee,
He having sworn against it), thou shalt have,
I bind it with my honour, satisfaction
To thine own wishes.

DOROTEA.

I desire no more, sir.
I have a witness, and a noble one
For truth and honesty.

PEDRO.

Go, bring him hither.

Exit DOROTEA.

FERNANDO.

    This lying boy will take him to his heels,
    And leave me slandered.

PEDRO.

                No; I'll be his voucher.

FERNANDO.

    Nay then, 'tis plain, this is confederacy.

PEDRO.

    That he has been an agent in your service
    Appears from this. Here is a letter, brother
    (Produced, perforce, to give him credit with me);
    The writing, yours; the matter, love, for so,
    He says, he can explain it.

DON CAMILLO.

               Then, belike,
    A young he-bawd.

FERNANDO.

            This forgery confounds me!

DUKE.

    Read it, Pedro.

PEDRO (*reads*).

    'Our prudence should now teach us to forget what our
    indiscretion has committed. I have already made one step
    towards this wisdom...'

FERNANDO.

    Hold, sir. (*Aside.*) My very words to Dorotea!

DUKE.

    Go on.

FERNANDO.

        My gracious father, give me pardon;
    I do confess I somesuch letter wrote
    (The purport all too trivial for your ear)
    But how it reached this young dissembler's hands,
    Is what I cannot solve. For on my soul,

And by the honours of my birth and house,
The minion's face till now I never saw.

PEDRO.

Run not too far in debt on protestation,
Why should you do a child this wrong?

FERNANDO.

Go to;

Your friendships past warrant not this abuse:
If you provoke me thus, I shall forget
What you are to me. This is mere practice
And villainy to draw me into scandal.

PEDRO.

No more; you are a boy. Here comes one
Shall prove you so: no more.

Enter CARDENIO.

Now, sir, whose practice breaks?

FERNANDO.

Another rascal!

FERNANDO *attacks* CARDENIO *but is beaten to the
ground.* GERARDO *attempts to intervene, but the* DUKE
holds him back.

DUKE.

Hold!

DON CAMILLO.

Now what's the matter!
What is he, lord? What is he?

PEDRO.

A certain son of yours.

DON CAMILLO.

The devil he is.

PEDRO.

If he be a devil, that devil must call you Father.

DON CAMILLO.

This almost melts me. Are you my poor lost boy?

CARDENIO (*in a whisper*).

Father...

CARDENIO *and* DON CAMILLO *embrace*.

PEDRO.

Gentle lady, what think you of this honest man?

LUSCINDA.

He has a face makes me remember something
I have thought well of: how he looks upon me!
Poor man, he weeps. Ha! stay; it cannot be,
He has his eye, his features, shape, and gesture.
Would he would speak...

CARDENIO.

Luscinda!

LUSCINDA.

Yes, 'tis he.

CARDENIO.

O Luscinda do I see thee there.

As LUSCINDA *and* CARDENIO *are about to embrace,
suddenly* FERNANDO, *sword in hand, leaps up and seizes*
LUSCINDA. *As he does so* DOROTEA *enters, dressed as a
woman. She throws herself at* FERNANDO's *feet.*

DOROTEA.

That sun thou hold'st eclipsed between thine arms,
So darkens and deprives thine eyes of sight
Thou canst not see here, prostrate at thy feet,
Disasterous Dorotea, and thy wife.

I am that humble country girl whom thou,
Or for thy bounty or thy pleasure, lord,
Didst deign to raise unto that giddy height
That she might call thee hers.

Yet for all this, I would not have you think
That guided by dishonourable steps,

I hither come, but conducted by dolour
To see my wretched self, forgot by thee.

Thou knowest upon what terms
I did subject myself unto thy will,
So that no place remains nor breath of doubt
To colour it a fraud or a deceit.

Know, my dear lord, that I do love thee still.
Matchless affections I do bear to thee.
Take them in recompense for her beauty,
That sun, for whom thou dost abandon me.

All this being so, as in verity it is,
Why dost thou, writhing so, delay to make
Mine ending happy, whose commencement thou
Didst wreathe with promises?

If thou wilt have me not for what I am,
Who am indeed thy true and lawful spouse,
Yet take me and admit me for thy slave;
For, so that I may be in thy possession,
I'll count myself forever fortunate.

Thou canst not be Luscinda's: thou art mine;
Nor she thine, forasmuch as she belongs
To her Cardenio. Reduce thy will
To love her that adores thee, than address
Her that hates thee.
Do not abandon me to my dishonour.

FERNANDO.
    She looks as beauteous and innocent
    As when I wronged her.

DOROTEA.
    And that which I will lastly say is this,
    Whether thou wilt or no, I am thy wife;
    The witnesses are thine own words declared,
    Which neither should nor ought to lie, my lord.

    And witness shall be also thine own hand.
    And witness Heaven, which thou didst invoke

To witness bear to what thou promised me.
And when all this shall fail, if this shall fail,
Thy very conscience then shall never fail
From using clamours, silent in thy mirth;
For this same truth which I have said to thee
Shall trouble all thy pleasure and delight.

FERNANDO.

Virtuous Dorotea. Too good for me!
Dare you love a man so faithless as I?
Thou hast quite vanquished me;
It is not possible or to resist
Or to deny so many truths united.

Arise, lady,
She should not be prostrated at my feet,
Whose image I've erected in my mind.

I know you love me. Thus, thus, thus and thus,
I print my vow'd repentance on thy cheek:
Let all men read it there. My gracious father
Forgive, and make me rich with your consent:
This is my wife; no other would I choose
Were she a queen.

DON CAMILLO.

Here's a new change!

FERNANDO.

And fair Luscinda, from whose virgin arms
I forced my wronged friend, Cardenio,
O forgive me. Take home your holy vows.
Give them to him that has deserved them.

CARDENIO.

If pitiful Heaven be pleased and would,
At last now have thee take some ease, and rest,
Thou canst not take it more secure than here
Between these arms which now receive thee, girl.

LUSCINDA.

Let me cleave to the wall whose ivy I am.
Only death can blot him from my memory.

They embrace.

DON CAMILLO.

Now what's the matter?

PEDRO.

Let 'em alone; they're almost starved for kisses.

DON CAMILLO.

Stand forty foot off. No man troubles 'em
Much good may it do your hearts.

DON BERNARDO.

When lovers swear true faith, the listening angels
Stand on the golden battlements of Heaven
And waft their vows to the eternal throne.

DUKE.

E'en as you are, we'll join your hands together.
A providence above our power rules all.
Ask him forgiveness, boy.

CARDENIO.

He has it, sir.

FERNANDO.

Once more. my friend,
Share in a heart that never shall wrong thee more.
And brother –

PEDRO.

This embrace cuts off excuses.

DUKE.

I must, in part, repair my son's offence:
At your best leisure, Cardenio, know our court.
And Dorotea (for I know you now)

I have debt to pay: for your virtue's sake
Tho' your descent be low, call me your father.
A match drawn out of honesty and goodness
Is pedigree enough. Are you all pleased?

Gives her to FERNANDO.

DON CAMILLO.
  All.

FERNANDO *and* DON BERNARDO.
     All, sir.

CARDENIO.
       All.

DUKE.
            And I not least.
  We'll now return to court
  (And that short travel, and your loves completed,
  Shall, as I trust, for life restrain these wanderings):
  There the solemnity and grace I'll do
  Your several nuptials shall approve my joy,
  And make grieved lovers that your story read
  Wish true love's wanderings like yours succeed.

Both couples embrace each other again.

FERNANDO, *whilst he holds* DOROTEA, *looks at* CARDENIO.

End of play.

A Letter

To the reviser and adapter of *Double Falshood*.

Dear Lewis Theobald,

Forgive me for writing to you, but I am rather a fan of yours. You are the man who claimed to have brought to light Shakespeare's lost play, *Cardenio*. If that is true, you deserve a place in the pantheon of great Shakespearians. If it's not true, you have certainly sent a lot of people on a very merry dance indeed.

Apparently you had more than one manuscript copy of *Cardenio* (although how many isn't clear), and you adapted it for the stage, as *Double Falshood; or The Distrest Lovers*. It opened at Drury Lane on 13 December 1727, and ran for ten consecutive performances.

The advertisement for the play which appeared in the *London Journal* read: 'This good old master is by a kind of miracle, recalled from his grave.' And when you printed the play, you chose a quotation from Virgil which might be translated as 'What the Gods themselves could not promise, revolving Time has brought to light.'

The discovery of a lost play by Shakespeare must indeed have seemed like some divinely inspired miracle, or were all these extravagant claims just part of the subterfuge?

I have a few questions I'd like to ask. Some years ago, I got a group of actors together to read your *Double Falshood*, at Stratford-upon-Avon, where there is now a company dedicated to producing the work of Shakespeare (you would have approved of that I think, Lewis). And although we greatly enjoyed it, we had some problems with it. We noticed that you had changed all the names from the original Cervantes' story (the source material), but more seriously, that there seem to be some missing scenes.

Why did you cut the scene where Don Fernando gets into Dorotea's room? Surely Shakespeare would have jumped at that scene: think of Iachimo and Imogen, or even Tarquin and Lucrece. And the scene where Fernando attempts to abduct Luscinda by being smuggled into a convent in a coffin? Jacobean drama is full of people leaping out of coffins, from Beaumont's quixotic *The Knight of the Burning Pestle*, to Middleton's *A Chaste Maid in Cheapside*, or Marston's *Antonio and Mellida*. That abduction scene must surely have existed in the original play.

You say you acquired a manuscript of *Cardenio* which was in the handwriting of John Downes, the famous old prompter from Drury Lane Theatre. Apparently the great tragedian, Thomas Betterton, was to have 'ushered the play into the world' after the Restoration. His company had already mounted adaptations of *Henry VIII* and *The Two Noble Kinsmen*, both plays in which Shakespeare is said to have collaborated with John Fletcher (although I know you will be surprised to learn that, Lewis). So it is feasible that they considered *Cardenio* for production. If so, it is highly probable that they would have adapted it. So perhaps these odd changes have nothing to do with you.

Of course it might be that the triumvirate of actor-managers who ran Drury Lane Theatre insisted on these changes. They had a reputation for being dismissive of new writing. How did you get on with them?

Robert Wilks, who was notoriously temperamental, was said to have been jealous of his rival, the theatre's leading tragic actor, Barton Booth, and neither of them much cared for plays in which they had to play second fiddle. Might this have been why you changed the title from *Cardenio* to *Double Falshood*? That way Wilks could play the irresistible villain, and Booth the hero figure, Cardenio, and neither's nose would be put out of joint. As Booth's wife Hester was playing the Dorotea role, together they must all have been able to exert a considerable amount of pressure for whatever changes they required.

I read that you had a disaster on opening night. One of your leads was off. Barton Booth hadn't been well and suffered a relapse. I can imagine the stress. It's your big break. Your play is about to open in one of the two major London theatres, with arguably one of the greatest actors of the day, and instead an understudy goes on. You begged Booth to go back into the show. He did, but he was seriously ill, and when he played the role on 9 January 1728, it turned out to be his last appearance on the stage. His wife never forgave you, did she?

Double Falshood was part of your master plan, wasn't it? I feel for you. Since giving up a career in the law, you had tried everything: classical translation, poetry, opera libretto. You even tried publishing a magazine (which folded) and a novel (which flopped). You were desperate to make it on the literary scene. You had even tried adapting Shakespeare, attempting to apply the classical unities to *Richard II,* and cutting about a thousand lines. It was not a success.

But you had found a lucrative niche writing pantomimes, which were all the rage in the 1720s, but I think your real ambition was to make your mark with Shakespeare. In 1725 you got your chance. The great poet of the Augustan age, and your exact contemporary, Alexander Pope, published his edition of Shakespeare. Not only did you regard it as sloppy and inaccurate, you disliked his tendency to correct Shakespeare's rhyme and improve his metre. So you published your response: *Shakespeare Restored* in 1726. Pope had a vicious wit, and satire was the rage of the age, so you must have known what an audacious step this was! About as risky today as talking on *Private Eye*.

But attacking Pope was just step one of this master plan, and it put you on the map as a '*Bard-dei defensor*'. Step Two: to secure your place in the pantheon of Shakespeare idolaters, your *coup de théâtre* was to produce a lost Shakespeare play.

How did you feel when the plan backfired?

Pope then published a poem called *The Dunciad*, about all the stupid dull people in London, and made you King of the Dunces. I don't want to rub it in, Lewis, but he referred to you as 'Piddling Tibbald'; and it was the title with which you were consigned to the footnotes of literary history for the next three centuries, I'm afraid. Pope smarted at the way you, a mere jumped-up writer of pantomimes, should dare to criticise him. But in fact your scrupulous precision would stand you in good stead in the future.

The Dunciad would charge you with jumping on a Shakespeare bandwagon for your own self-glorification:

> *Yet even this creature may some notice claim*
> *Wrapt round and sanctified with Shakespeare's name*

You did get to publish your own edition of Shakespeare in the end, and for one brilliant deduction in particular you deserve our lasting thanks. Mrs Quickly has a baffling line in the Folio about the death of Falstaff in *Henry V*: 'For his nose was as sharp as a pen, and a table of green fields.' Pope suggested this was a stage direction; that a table was brought on stage, belonging to a man called Greenfield, who must have been the property-man at the Globe. But instead, you had the happy felicity to realise that Falstaff might in his last moments, have 'babbled o' green fields': sublime! 'Shakespeare Restored' indeed.

You would be pleased to know that you are now widely considered to be one of the great Shakespeare editors of the eighteenth century.

William Hogarth painted you as 'The Distrest Poet' (punning on the subtitle of your play) and you died in poverty in 1744.

Only one person attended your funeral, your old friend, the prompter, John Stede. But he left us a sketch of your character: 'He was of a generous spirit, too generous for his circumstances, and none knew how to do a handsome thing... with a better grace than himself.'

Now, Lewis, nearly two hundred and seventy years after your death, controversy over *Double Falshood* continues, with some debate about whether it was a forgery after all. The manuscript that might have proved it, that was reported as late as 1770 as being 'treasured up in the museum Covent Garden Playhouse', was probably destroyed when that theatre burnt down in 1808.

My own opinion? Well, I think you were fiercely ambitious, but I think you also loved Shakespeare too much to foist a total fabrication on the world (although I notice you didn't include the play in your own later edition of Shakespeare's works). And your knowledge of the law would suggest you would not have risked exposure! I think you inherited a script that had already been prepared for presentation in the Restoration period, and you tidied it up a bit. But within it is still preserved some Shakespeare DNA.

We should be cautious about attempting to recreate a Shakespeare play from that DNA: that would be like cloning dinosaurs in *Jurassic Park* (sorry, Lewis, you won't understand that reference), but we can perhaps fill in the gaps in that genetic code, and use your script to re-imagine, with the help of Cervantes' original story, what such a play might have been like.

So thanks, Lewis. We'll raise a glass in your memory. And if you are watching, enjoy the play.

Greg Doran

Gregory Doran's book *Shakespeare's Lost Play: Re-imagining* Cardenio *for the Royal Shakespeare Company* will be published by Nick Hern Books later in the year. To reserve your copy go to www.nickhernbooks.co.uk

'Wood, Rocks and Mountains'

The historian and television documentarist Michael Wood
discovered a new piece of the *Cardenio* jigsaw when he was
working on his BBC series *In Search of Shakespeare* in 2001.
He uncovered in the British Library, an anonymous set of lyrics
among the papers of Robert Johnson (1583–1633), the King's
lutenist, and composer for some of Shakespeare's late plays. The
song 'Woods, Rocks and Mountains', could well be a setting
from the original production of *Cardenio* of Dorotea's song in
Act Four among the shepherds in the Sierra Morena.

In the end in our production, our composer Paul Englishby and
I chose to set the words in Theobald's adaptation *Double
Falshood* instead ('Fond Echo'), as Johnson's Jacobean setting
– although very beautiful – did not suit our heightened Spanish
setting. However, we decided to include them here as an
alternative. A facsimile of the music score is available in Brean
Hammond's edition of *Double Falshood* for the Arden
Shakespeare.

Woods, rocks and mountains, and you desert places,
Where nought but bitter cold and hunger dwells,
Hear a poor maid's last words, killed with disgraces,
Slide softly while I sing you silver fountains
And let your hollow waters like sad bells
Ring, ring to my woes while miserable I
Cursing my fortunes, drop a tear and die.

A Nick Hern Book

Cardenio first published in this edition in Great Britain in 2011 as a paperback original by Nick Hern Books Limited, 14 Larden Road, London W3 7ST, in association with the Royal Shakespeare Company

This adaptation of *Cardenio* copyright © 2011 Gregory Doran with Antonio Álamo

Gregory Doran and Antonio Álamo have asserted their moral rights to be identified as the authors of this work

Cover image by RSC/Dusthouse with Oliver Rix as Cardenio
Cover design by Ned Hoste, 2H

Typeset by Nick Hern Books, London
Printed and bound in Great Britain by CLE Print Ltd, St Ives, Cambs PE27 3LE

A CIP catalogue record for this book is available from the British Library

ISBN 978 1 84842 180 6